"GIMME A HUG"

How Small Acts of Recognition Deliver Big Results and Create a Culture of Success

GEORGE KOURI

MILNER & ASSOCIATES INC
· EDITING · PUBLISHING · COMMUNICATIONS · CONSULTING ·

Copyright © 2014, by George Kouri

All rights reserved. No part of this work covered by the copyright herein may be reproduced or used in any form or by any means—graphic, electronic, or mechanical—without the prior written permission of the author. Any request for photocopying, recording, taping or information storage and retrieval systems of any part of this book shall be directed in writing to the Canadian Copyright Licensing Agency (Access Copyright). For an Access Copyright license, visit www.accesscopyright.ca or call toll-free 1-800-893-5777.

Care has been taken to trace ownership of copyright material contained in this book. The publisher will gladly receive any information that will enable them to rectify any reference or credit line in subsequent editions.

This publication is designed to provide accurate and authoritative information in regard to the subject matter covered. It is sold on the understanding that the publisher is not engaged in rendering professional services. If professional advice or other expert assistance is required, the services of a competent professional should be sought.

Library and Archives Canada Cataloguing in Publication

Kouri, George, 1943-, author
           "Gimme a hug" : how small acts of recognition deliver big results and create a culture of success / George Kouri.

Issued in print and electronic formats.
ISBN 1502759160   - ISBN 13: 9781502759160

           1. Incentive awards.   2. Employee motivation.   I. Title.

HF5549.5.I5K68 2014   658.3'142   C2014-905497-1
                                         C2014-905498-X

Production Credits
Editor: Karen Milner
Interior design and typesetting: Adrian So
Cover design: Adrian So

Published by Milner & Associates Inc.
www.milnerassociates.ca

Praise for *"Gimme a Hug,"* and for George Kouri

"George knows that inspired people build business success. He has spent his career coaching business people—building their confidence and stretching their minds to think outside the box. This book reflects many of his personal thoughts and passions developed over his decades of commitment to people."
— *Mr. Brian Arbique, Managing Director, Heinz Canada*

"Thank you for the positive influence you have had on my entire career. Your advice and guidance contributed greatly to my advancement and my success. You made me a better leader. You are a man of great merit."
— *Mr. Robert Depatie, CEO Quebecor*

"I consider myself very fortunate for having met you. You have helped me grow and become a better human being. For that, I am deeply grateful to you. Thank you for your unconditional support and coaching."
— *Ms. Naseem Somani, CEO Gamma-Dynacare Medical Laboratories*

"Hey George, you are an amazing person. I learned so much from you. Thank you for the insights, wisdom, and expertise. You've helped make a difference in my life and I'm grateful for that."
— *Ms. Candace S. Simerson, President/Chief Operating Officer, Minnesota Eye Consultants, PA*

"George, thank you so very much. I really appreciate your coaching and guidance. It has meant the world to me. I feel so fortunate to have you in my life. You taught me how to release the compassion and power that were locked inside of me, giving me the greatest gift — being able to help others. Always thinking of you my friend."
— *Mr. Paul Crawford, President, Solex Thermal Science Inc.*

"I truly value your advice and appreciate the guidance you have given to help me. I know for years to come, when faced with various situations, I will refer to the acronym that we created — WWGD — 'What Would George Do?'. Sincere thanks to you for being an awesome coach."
— *Ms. Mary Holbrook, Director, Human Resources, Autodata Solutions Inc.*

My biggest hugs are for Marlene

CONTENTS

Chapter 1:	What's This "Hug" Stuff All About?	1
Chapter 2:	Recognition and Rejection	11
Chapter 3:	The Power of Recognition in the Workplace	27
Chapter 4:	The Process of Recognition	37
Chapter 5:	Easy Ways to Give Others Recognition	53
Chapter 6:	Stop Rejecting, Start Coaching	61
Chapter 7:	How to Manage Mistakes	71
Chapter 8:	Zero Tolerance for Bullies	85
Chapter 9:	Establish a No-Bullies Policy	95
Chapter 10:	The Human Files	107
Chapter 11:	Simple Truths for Managing People	121
Chapter 12:	Manage How Others Perceive You	149
Chapter 13:	Finding the Balance between Right and Wrong	159
Chapter 14:	The Perfectionist's Prison	171
Chapter 15:	Be a Leader — Demonstrate Leadership	185
Chapter 16:	Managing the Voice	195
Chapter 17:	Boost Your Own Self-Confidence	201
Chapter 18:	Make "Why Not?" Your Strategic Focus	205
Chapter 19:	What Would Your License Plate Say?	211
Chapter 20:	My Best Friend, George	213
"Gimme a Hug"		217
Acknowledgments		219
About the Author		223

1

WHAT'S THIS "HUG" STUFF ALL ABOUT?

"All I ever wanted in my life was a hug."

That's the refrain I've heard, in one form or another, from the hundreds of people I've had the honor to help in my 35 years as an executive coach. It is the prime need I've listened to. Of course, it wasn't a physical hug they craved, but rather a metaphorical one. It was an expression of their thirst to be acknowledged for their value, their worth, their contributions, and their achievements.

It was a statement that encapsulated the true feelings they've had, as children growing up, as students, as employees, and as managers and executives. Their need for a "hug" was also an expression of the profound frustration and emptiness they felt, no matter how successful they were, no matter what position they had, and no matter how high they had climbed the ladder of life.

Our coaching sessions helped these people understand this underlying need, its various manifestations, its complexities and, of course, the how-to techniques they could use to manage and control this need for a "hug."

My purpose was to help them enjoy a far more satisfying and rewarding career as well as a far more satisfying personal life. My focus was on helping them understand and apply simple methods and techniques that would enable them to better manage themselves, better manage others, and better manage the numerous and varied aspects of their work.

They were able to appreciate the fact that they really were better than they thought they were. Our sessions enabled them to realize the vast scope of their skills, their talents, their goodness, and their value. As a result, they were able to achieve more, to reach new levels of success, and to attain new levels of satisfaction. Their confidence skyrocketed and, as a result, so did their accomplishments.

Learning to give and to receive metaphorical "hugs" really did enable them to be better than they had given themselves credit for, or, more to the point, than they had been recognized for by their circle of family, friends, and employers.

Coaching helped them learn a lot about themselves. That unleashed a powerhouse of goodness that they were then able to share with others around them.

As an illustration of what that means, here's a note I recently received from one of the individuals I have had the honor to coach. He's the President of a large, worldwide organization:

> *"I feel so fortunate to have you in my life. You taught me how to release the compassion and power that were locked inside of me—giving me the greatest gift—being able to help others. Thanks. Always thinking of you, my friend."*
> — Paul C.

The power of helping others; the power of recognizing others; the power of caring about others; the power of making others feel good; the power of inspiring others, of teaching others, of acknowledging them; the power of thanking them, of just being nice to them—of being able to give them a "hug" is immense. It's far more rewarding than one can imagine, far more satisfying, and far more nourishing than people realize.

Paul is just one example of this power, of being able to make things better for others. In doing so, Paul himself became a better manager and has derived a much higher level of satisfaction from his work. And here's the other benefit he derived—the employee he "hugged" was inspired by Paul's leadership. And because of that, she became a much better manager of her department.

This book is designed to explain the various aspects of how this need for a hug manifests itself, its very essence, its various dimensions, its complexities, the various disguises it hides behind, and how to manage and deal with it to make yourself and the people you interact with better and more fulfilled in many ways. I want you to reap the immense rewards that you will generate and I want you to do that in simple and easy-to-apply methods. Methods that work. I'll continue to use the "hug" metaphor because it's easy to remember and, once you learn the techniques, you'll realize it is very simple to apply.

The first and most important realization is that no one is just going to come up to you and ask for a hug, nor are they going to come up to you and give you an actual, physical hug. And you're not likely to go to someone you work with and ask for a hug. So we're all in this "hug zone" and no one is making, or about to make, a move to get or to give "a hug." Yet, and here's the key point, everyone wants and needs a hug. That's an indisputable fact that can never be refuted.

Here are some other indisputable facts, particular to the business world:

- Every company and every manager wants a high level of productivity.
- Companies want to have a "high-performance culture."
- They want to have a "do-it-right-the-first-time" culture.
- They want to minimize mistakes.
- They want their people to focus on satisfying customers' needs.
- They want high-quality production.
- They want to be known as the "go-to company" in their field of endeavor.
- They want creativity and initiative from their people.
- They want dedication, accountability, responsibility from their employees.

They want to generate the highest possible bottom-line results, the more profits the better.

No one is about to argue or diminish any of these goals, objectives and principles. They are the essence of any successful business. But what might surprise you is that this "hug thing" is one of the keys to achieving all of these outcomes and what keeps the company running. What keeps people running, so to speak, the fuel that drives people to high levels of achievement and gives them incredible satisfaction, even greatness, is this same need for "a hug."

So, if you want to bring out the best in yourself, if you want to discover and bring out the hidden skills and talents you definitely have and use them to greater advantage, please give serious consideration to this "hug" thing we're talking about. After all, why just settle for your own status quo when you can attain so much more out of life and out of your relationships?

For those who feel the need to reinvent themselves, to embark on a new career, or just to add new dimensions to their life, please note that this "hug" thing is a major key that unlocks the power to do all this. You can be better in every aspect of your life. You can achieve more, get more, be happier, be more fulfilled, realize your full potential, overcome your fears, and elevate your self-confidence and your self-esteem. That's what this book is all about.

All the techniques in here have been used with great results for the people who implemented them in both their business and personal life. So please read and re-read every section of this book—and enjoy the rewards you'll generate from applying these simple how-to methods.

So how do we go about achieving all these business and personal objectives?

Give a Hug, Get a Hug

This is the easiest, simplest how-to formula you'll ever learn about and the easiest to put into your daily routine, at home and at work. Let's go over it.

The one sure thing that I've learned in all my years as an executive coach is that,

- by *first* giving to others;
- by *first* doing for others;
- by *first* helping others;
- by *first* caring about others;
- by *first* making a positive impact on others;

They in turn will thank you. They will express their appreciation to you for the help you have given them. They will make you feel great because you made them feel great; they will make you feel wanted because you made them feel wanted; they will make you feel valued because you made them feel valued and appreciated *first*. In other words, they will give you a "hug" because you first gave them a "hug"—the "hug" that you needed too.

The effect of receiving thanks and recognition from others you help is amazing. And the formula for getting that metaphorical "hug" is very simple:

- *First* say or do something nice for someone else.
- *First* make others feel great.
- *First* compliment them.
- *First* acknowledge their hard work.
- *First* recognize the effort they put into a project.
- *First* help them, care for them.

And presto—they will give you a "hug" in return.

The rest of this book is designed to explain the various aspects of how this formula works, at work, at home, everywhere. The numerous examples we'll talk about will demonstrate how small acts of recognition—those hugs we've been talking about—deliver big results and create a culture of success.

Here are just a few small acts of recognition to consider:

- Express thanks to your people and to the people in other departments for their help, their contributions, and their efforts
- Discover and pay attention to the needs, desires, hobbies, passions of your employees and show them your interest
- Be on the lookout for the good things your people do, even the smallest things, and express your appreciation
- Make the time to listen to what they have to say, the good or not so good things they may want to talk about
- Engage your people by asking for their input and their viewpoints on various aspects of the business

- Keep information flowing to your people so that they feel involved and are important contributors to the success of the business
- Constantly update your people on the goals and achievements of the department
- Demonstrate an interest in their personal lives, especially their children
- Be proactive in matters, such as medical and health appointments they have and allow them to leave early or take time off
- Acknowledge all overtime and extra work done by your people
- Greet everyone you see with a smile and a pleasant comment

In other words, focus on the small acts of recognition that can make a big, positive difference to your people, that show them that you care and are paying attention to them.

In the work environment, far too many supervisors who have people management responsibilities have never attended what I like to call, the "hug" school of people management. You can tell that because they spew out the following statements, which I have listened to for years:

They get paid—they should be lucky to have a job. My job is to make sure they generate great results. If they do, they keep their job; if they don't, they get shuffled off out of here. That's what I believe people management is all about.

Business? Listen here GK, my priority is to get the quarter in and that's all. Around here its quarter-by-quarter results—nothing else matters. And besides, the people thing is HR's responsibility, not mine.

So, buzz off GK—I'm not in the "hug" business.

Sad but true. Sad because they just don't realize the powerful force of recognition and the major role it plays in generating positive bottom-line results and all the good things a manager wants to achieve.

So I'm not going to "buzz off," as one manager told me to do. Instead, I want to share some thoughts, observations, and techniques with you, based on the fascinating experiences and the incredible results I've had in my 35 years of helping people. I trust they will help you to become a better manager and even a better person, one who drives tremendous business results and derives great personal rewards.

As a point of reference, and before we go on, you should know that my business career began as soon as I graduated from McGill University in business and psychology. I was fortunate enough to get a job as a sales representative with Johnson & Johnson. Actually I kind of "influenced" my way into the job because I offered to work for free for the first three months in order to prove that I would be a great employee. After all, I had no experience as a sales person, in fact, no experience in business at all. I didn't even know how to drive a car at that point, something I hadn't considered when I applied for the sales job. But when you're as desperate as I was, you take risks, you go for it, you learn quickly, and you become inventive.

A few days after offering to work for free for three months, I got the job—and so began my career at Johnson & Johnson. I was with them for 15 years in various sales, marketing, and business development positions, making it up to the executive level. I then left to start my own business in executive coaching.

Thirty-five years later, I have been very fortunate, and blessed, to have coached people in all kinds of professions, in all walks of life, and at all levels of an organization. I've worked with blue-chip companies, start-ups, associations, legal firms, volunteer groups, and many others. I've coached the same people for years and helped them develop and grow their careers. It's been very satisfying to see the incredibly positive power of the "hug" in action with these people. Their reward was to elevate themselves from one position to the next higher one, several becoming the CEO of their company. This "hug" stuff really worked for them—and it will work for you.

I've counselled countless children of my clients, which I do with my compliments. I've always had a special place in my heart for kids and teens. I love to help them get through their special challenges and help them find their way in life and in their career. That special place for kids is due to the fact that no one ever came to my aid when I needed help. I was an orphan in many ways, so I'm very happy to extend myself to help others, especially children.

I've also helped save hundreds of people's careers because their bosses didn't know how to manage them and couldn't or didn't want to see the individual's potential. It's so tragic to see people in supervisory and management positions who do not have a clue about how to manage people.

In addition, I've brought a countless number of teams together and helped them work better together, achieve more together and be enriched by winning and succeeding together. It's an absolute joy to see a group of people go from just hearing their own individual voice to hearing the voices of others. The sound of the "team" is so much more beautiful and far more powerful.

I've worked with hundreds of executive teams and helped them deal with various situations: strategic development, career management, people management, employee surveys, succession planning, corporate culture changes, and on and on.

I've had the privilege of coaching people in fields as diverse as the following:

- Salespeople
- Accountants
- Sales Managers
- Lawyers
- Marketing Managers
- Secretaries
- Nurses
- Assistants
- Architects
- Production-Line Workers
- Engineers
- Financial Advisors
- General Practitioners
- Foremen
- Cardiologists
- CEOs
- NHL Hockey Players
- Psychoanalysts

- Principal Ballet Dancers
- Plant Managers
- Presidents

I've helped people understand who they are and what they are and helped them move forward and get on with managing their work, their relationships, and their life. That's what this book is all about. It's taking the experiences and fulfilment of 35 years of helping people and putting them down on paper so that they can help others.

I know many readers, especially in the world of business, may be a little put off by the whole idea of "hugging" people as a management style, even if the hug is a metaphorical one. But what you will find in this book is a lot of practical, how-to advice that you can use immediately to improve any and all of your relationships—at work, at home, wherever.

Perhaps what you read will provoke you out of your normal, day-to-day comfort zone. But bear with it, this is all stuff that has worked for countless people before you. And there are some easy-to-use formulas that really work.

The other important point that I think is essential to note is that nothing in this book preaches a change in your personality or your character. You are who you are. You have the habits you have. Your being, your essence, was set in stone a long time ago. I'm not out to change that.

It's important to note that you really can't change a person. All I try to do is to help them modify behaviors, teach them new techniques, and open their eyes to different ways of managing the two basic elements of human interaction—what to say and what to do. You can teach someone how to write, how to speak, how to overcome fears, how to manage challenges and so on. You can inspire and motivate and build confidence—but deep down their psychology is set in stone.

So we're not out to change anyone, just to enlighten people and expose them to new thoughts. What I'd like you to think about is that if—and it's a big IF—you want to improve the way you manage others or interact with colleagues; if you want to get out of the rut that you may be in; if you want to re-energize yourself or even re-invent yourself, as many try to do; or even if you just want to introduce a new perspective into your life, read on.

And here's the most important benefit of all: If you want to bring out the best in yourself, if you want to discover and bring out the hidden skills and talents you definitely have and use them to greater advantage, then read and re-read every section of this book.

There are simple techniques in this book that you probably have never even thought of, let alone applied, in your day-to-day existence. It contains tried and true how-to methods and principles that have actually been used with my clients, with great success.

As I write, I actually see you sitting in front of me and we're just having a chat about things, much as I have done in my coaching sessions with clients. Consider this book a casual conversation between us, but one with a very important message that can help to modify various aspects of both your work life and your personal life for the better and, in doing so, enable you to achieve greater fulfillment and a heightened sense of satisfaction.

So, let's get into it.

2

RECOGNITION AND REJECTION

I want to start off by talking about what I believe are the two most important words to help everyone understand people better. Two simple words that are at the heart of managing and interacting with people effectively—at work, at home, everywhere. Two simple words that are "foundational" when it comes to:

- Managing a variety of personal and business relationships
- Creating a positive working environment
- Becoming a great leader
- Becoming a great communicator
- Being a very successful person
- Being a great parent

And learning about and managing yourself and your life—better.

What has been confirmed to me, over and over again, is that people in all walks of life, whoever they might be, whatever position they may have, whatever title is on their business cards, operate under the two umbrellas of **Recognition** and **Rejection**.

In all of its dimensions, in all of its aspects, and even in all of its perplexities, **Recognition** has proven to be the prime motivator of people, the prime driver of human initiative, and the prime force that pushes people to generate incredible achievements.

On the other hand, **Rejection** is the prime destructive force. It destroys people; it destroys relationships of all kinds; it destroys confidence; it inhibits initiatives; and, in its ugliest form, drives people to depression and hopelessness, which in turn drives them to say and do bad things—some very bad things.

In the business world, rejection shows its ugly face directly on the bottom line, primarily because employees who feel rejected cannot perform at their best. Poor employee morale always leads to poor performance and poor performance always has a direct impact on the productivity and profitability of the organization—and that impact is always negative. When your people feel rejected:

- They withdraw.
- They do the minimum.
- They become ambivalent.
- You witness all kinds of negative behaviors like being late, leaving early.
- They're not engaged in the business.
- They are not active participants at meetings.
- They don't contribute ideas for the betterment of the business.
- There is a definite deficiency of initiative and creativity.
- They complain and whine about everything.
- Their cup is always empty, never mind being just half full.
- They are not team players, never going out of their way to help others.
- They always have an excuse for not getting involved.
- They do not and cannot operate to their full potential.
- Their confidence and self-esteem are at rock-bottom levels.
- They are prime candidates for dismissal.

The list can be extended for sure, but it proves the point that rejection, in all of its dimensions, is an extremely destructive force that inhibits the growth and prosperity of a company and its people. And the other important manifestation of rejection in the workplace is the dissatisfaction that employees feel. In fact, their number-one complaint is that they don't feel appreciated by their superiors. Yes, it's the number-one complaint, not money or other material things.

Outside of the work environment, rejection is even more destructive, especially when it begins in early childhood. What needs to be understood is that a major vacuum is created and the individual has no choice but to be on the hunt to fill that vacuum. Work, for many, is potentially an excellent place to do that. However, if the person happens to work for a boss who dishes out more rejection than praise, poor performance will become a serious issue, inevitably leading to the firing of that person. His or her search for recognition will continue at another company.

What's significant here is that the rejection they endure erodes whatever confidence they may have had. And low confidence results in low performance. These people don't seem to get anywhere in their careers. They are constantly looking for their confidence to be enlivened, to be appreciated, and yes, to be hugged, to fill the void that they have carried with them since early childhood.

Sadly, rather than realizing their full potential, they jump from one job to another, in their quest to fill the vacuum that eats away at them. Decades later, they are still doing the same work, never advancing or taking on new responsibilities. And the shame of it is that they usually are very smart people. They have the knowledge to achieve great things, but they can't because of the destructive force of rejection.

Here's another perspective for your consideration. I've always believed that when a child feels rejected and unloved at home, they may very well turn to things like gangs, and drugs, and alcohol to try to find some comfort, some form or other of recognition. Perhaps not always, and not all kids—but many do.

It's an important point, so let me expand on it. For example, gangs are a great place to feel wanted, appreciated, and in a strange way, loved. I know because I joined a gang as a teenager and felt fantastic about it. It filled the void created by the daily barrage of hearing, "You're nothing but a piece of garbage. You'll never amount to anything."

The Speck Gang welcomed me with open arms. They made me feel wanted; I was a "somebody," I was important, I belonged. Incredible, but

I really felt appreciated and even "loved" in some way, even if it was a warped sense of the traditional definition of the word "love."

I was not abused in the gang, like I was at home. In the gang we laughed together, we played jokes on each other. I never heard a put-down, I was never verbally abused, never physically abused. We had team spirit in every sense of the word. If you needed to talk, a gang member was there to listen, to help you out; he had your back. No questions were asked, no judgments were made. There was a sense of freedom. You had everything you wanted and, if the gang didn't have it, they would help you get it, usually not in a legal way, but you got it—and that felt terrific. You were supported, encouraged, and protected. Your confidence, your self-esteem were enlivened.

In fact, that's what the major responsibility of every manager should be: to support, encourage, and build the confidence of his or her people. That's why it's so important to get into the habit of rewarding, rather than rejecting. As I mentioned earlier, it just takes small acts of recognition to motivate and inspire your people to achieve great performance.

The gang environment did that, despite the terrible reputation that gangs have. It's where I discovered I had a very creative streak in me. I discovered how important it was to really make a difference in what you do, to take initiative, and to constantly be on the look-out for new opportunities, even though those new opportunities were not generally prescribed by society. It didn't matter; you sought them out, you went after them because you knew you'd get the recognition you needed and the attention of your gang buddies.

I felt powerful. I felt validated. And in that environment, I truly believed I could do anything—nothing stood in my way, nothing! I even rose to be the leader of the gang. It was my first leadership position.

I finally understood the attraction of gangs. After all, if you spend your childhood years being abused and rejected at home, you seek to be appreciated and recognized. And, frankly, it doesn't matter who gives you the "hug" you so badly needed.

Now imagine the power and the satisfaction you would have as a manager, if you could make someone feel appreciated, feel valuable, and feel recognized for what they did, for what they said, for their efforts, and for their contributions and accomplishments. In fact, this book shows you throughout how you can do exactly that, by adopting some simple but powerful ways of giving your people what they really need to create a high-performance team.

The Two Most Powerful Forces

The key point is that Recognition and Rejection are two very powerful forces, seemingly obvious, but so overlooked and so misunderstood. I fervently believe that these two words help to explain human behavior and that they are at the foundation of why people say and do what they say and do—and why they behave as they do.

Come on GK, that's just too simple. You can't explain human behavior and how to manage people with just those two words, can you? My answer is a resounding, "YES!"

Why complicate things when they really are simple and easy to understand? The fact is there are too many fancy formulas and theories about human behavior that just add confusion to the subject and make it appear to be so complex.

Here's an easy test to prove the point. Do you like being rejected? I'm sure your answer is "no." Let's look at the other side of the coin. Do you like to be appreciated? I'm sure your answer is "yes." Point made. It's simple. It's easy to understand. Yet I have seen so many companies spend millions to send their people on courses that supposedly help in their understanding of "people management."

There are programs that assign colours to people: red/blue, green/yellow, and so on. Some companies even post the colours of the individual on the door of their office. Before you walk into their office, you know they are a blue/green and that is supposed to help you deal with the individual. Really?

Other programs classify people with numbers, all in the hope of defining who and what people are. That's fine. If you feel better knowing that you're a 1/9 or a 9/1, or whatever, enjoy—but don't for a second forget the two most powerful words: Recognition and Rejection.

What I've learned is that people share one thing in common: They all want to be recognized and appreciated; they do not like to be rejected or put-down. Understanding people is that simple. And that has been proven to me by the hundreds and hundreds of people I've coached over the past 35 years.

If you want to understand what makes people tick, just think about what the people around you felt being recognized, or being rejected, by you in your role as a parent, as a manager, as a friend. And of course, ask yourself how you felt when you were recognized or rejected.

It's very simple. People want to hear a kind word, a thoughtful phrase like "thank you," or "that was nice of you to do that," "I really appreciated the fact that you came in on the weekend to finish that assignment," and so on. For some reason, we seem to have lost, forgotten, or taken those phrases, and many others, for granted. Let me share with you some of the exact quotes I've heard:

I want to be treated like a human being, not a number.

I worked my butt off all weekend long. I had to miss my daughter's performance in the school play. No one around here noticed; they don't give a damn. You never hear a kind word or a simple thank-you from anyone. People don't matter anymore.

The only thing my boss does is point out the things I didn't do well. He's never once given me a compliment or said thanks. I'm tired of being yelled at like a little child.

The style of management around here is "dictate and control." Everyone hates it and they're all looking for jobs. Why don't they get rid of him? These are good people who really like the company but hate the boss.

Why bother saying anything? They don't care. They won't do anything about it; if you say anything, you just get shot down and are labelled as negative.

I don't think anyone that I know is complaining about money or stuff like that. They just want to be treated with respect and be recognized for the hard work they do.

I just want to be talked to in a respectful manner, not in a manner that makes me feel small and insignificant.

I'm not sure that management really cares about people. They seem to be more concerned with their stock options than they are about the people who actually get the work done. It gets done but there's a lot of stress getting it done.

People seem to be more concerned about titles and status than about helping each other. You often hear, "That's not my job. Get someone else to do that." It's always someone else's fault. It's ridiculous. How do you run a business without having a sense of responsibility?

There's a lot of intimidation around here. People are afraid to say anything; they know they'll get bullied if they do.

We have a finger-pointing culture around here.

No matter what I do, they're never pleased.

Those are real comments from real people. The simplest way to describe what I'm hearing—the real need that I believe is being expressed—is that people are simply saying, *"Gimme a hug."* Of course, this request, this need, is a metaphorical one, but deep down inside they are asking for some positive feedback.

In other words, people need to be recognized. They need to feel important. They need to sense that they are valued and appreciated. The fact is that in order to become a great manager and a great leader, it is vital to incorporate recognition into your day-to-day work life, and to make it, in all of its varieties, a key part of your management style. It should be effortless, routine. A great leader knows that this matter of "a hug" is really crucial to performance improvement, to employee satisfaction and to a highly productive and profitable business.

The Importance of Recognition

First: Recognition makes for good business metrics, the chief of which is a positive improvement to the bottom-line.

Second: We need to realize that acceptance, recognition, and appreciation are powerful motivators, and that motivated people achieve great things.

Third: Understand, or just accept, how deeply rooted the need for recognition is in every person's make-up. They're all saying the same thing, "Gimme a hug."

It is vital to understand and accept the fact that the need for recognition is profoundly and fundamentally rooted in every person's make-up:

- Children want the "love"—of their parents (recognition)
- Students want the "validation"—of their teacher (recognition)
- Employees want the "acceptance"—of their boss (recognition)
- Adults want the "respect"—of their community (recognition)

The need for recognition is so powerful that it can drive behavior in ways you may not even be aware of. For example, some very wealthy people donate huge sums of money to hospitals, universities, and other institutions, in order to give back to the community. What looks on the surface like a pure act of altruism is very often driven by the need for the benefactor to receive their own recognition. The organization promotes the donor's good works, erects plaques and even buildings in their name, providing them with the public recognition that, in turn, makes them feel as good as those to whom they donated the funds.

We should all be grateful that wealthy people do things like that because these are great and wonderful expressions and deeds of generosity. It's all good stuff. It helps people. So, thank you to all those who do this. It's very much appreciated.

The unassailable fact is that people need to be recognized, to feel important, to sense that they are valued, that they are making a contribution to the success of the company; that their boss recognizes the efforts and hard work they do; that their parents accept and love them unconditionally.

Because of its vital importance—and because it is so overlooked, taken for granted, or simply ignored—I want to ensure that we all understand that the definition of **Recognition** covers a lot of ground. I describe **Recognition** as a giant umbrella, under which we find the following:

- Acceptance
- Accolades

- Appreciation
- Approval
- Acknowledgment
- Encouragement
- Importance
- Praise
- Reassurance
- Respect
- Support
- Validation
- Worthiness

Look over the list several times—get familiar with it—and then start demonstrating what the words mean to the people you come in contact with, whether you're a boss, a parent, a friend, a member of a team—whatever.

> **Recognition: The Heart of the Matter**
>
> Recognition is at the heart of creating meaningful and lasting relationships.
>
> Recognition is at the heart of raising children and building their confidence.
>
> Recognition is at the heart of having a more fulfilling life for you and your family.
>
> Recognition is at the heart of nourishing your own personal needs for satisfaction and appreciation and worthiness, even self-actualization.
>
> Recognition is at the heart of creating and leaving a vibrant and positive legacy.

Every single person I've coached needed some form or other of recognition, and directed their life in such a manner that they would get it. They needed to feel important. They wanted approval, validation, and they worked like heck to get it.

As a result of my experiences with these people, and the evidence I've gathered over the years, I've come to the conclusion and the realization that acceptance and appreciation, and all the other words under the "recognition umbrella" are extremely powerful motivators—motivators that drive people to achieve great things. Here are some real examples:

> *Naseem went from being an accountant to becoming the CEO of a major company in the health-care industry, all because she vowed to make her father proud of her.*
>
> *Andy drives himself so hard, and is achieving great things in the digital media business, because he is still trying to change the badgering sound of his father's voice into the sound of appreciation.*
>
> *Paul lived in the shadow of his siblings, never allowed to express himself as he would have liked to. It wreaked havoc with his self-confidence and only after many coaching sessions did he realize just how talented he really was.*
>
> *Robert was selling tomato juice when his boss asked me to start coaching him. He saw a spark in him. Our coaching sessions turned that spark into a fireworks display that was amazing. Today he is the CEO of a major communications company and has proven to his parents that he has achieved greatness.*

Real people, driving themselves to achieve and hence to be recognized for it. Amazingly, they're all fundamentally saying the same thing, "Gimme a hug." Their quest for acceptance, validation, and recognition has driven them to achieve greatness, not only for themselves, but also because they have an acute sensitivity to this "hug" thing, for the people who work with them.

Take Action: Give Your First Hug. Now.

To prove just how easy it is to give someone recognition and appreciation, stop reading this right now and give somebody a "hug." Of course I don't mean you should jump up and throw your arms around someone at the office, but rather, give someone a metaphorical hug.

To help you take this important first step, I'll show you how easy and simple this is. First, think about the people on your own team and then those in other departments. Consider such questions as the following:

- Have they been helpful to the team?
- Have they met your expectations?

- Have they performed in a positive manner?
- Have they gone out of their way to advance the business?
- Have they worked late to finish a project or to complete the report you needed?
- Have they gone above and beyond in any aspect of their work?
- Have they done something that really impressed you?
- Have people in other departments saved your bacon?

In other words, look for the good stuff in your team members and in the people in other departments. A little hint that may help you do this: think of the past few days or the week that has just gone by and focus on the positive contributions of the people, not the spectacular, just the good stuff that helped move things forward—and often that is just effort.

If you've played team sports, you know exactly what that means. The players are always "high-fiving" each other for a good effort, tapping each other on the behind for a good tackle or a good pass. Just watch a sports event on TV and you'll see what I mean. The players are focused on the good stuff that their team members are doing, because they know that if they show their team members small acts of recognition—that "hug" stuff we've been talking about—it will result in spectacular results and will create a team that wins.

A few minutes on your part to consider the good stuff that the people around you are doing is all it takes. You'll be amazed at all the good stuff you'll discover, be that results, efforts, team engagement, special contributions, idea generation, participation at a meeting, helping a team member, doing something special, going out of their way for the team, the department, whatever.

Now, take a moment to express your appreciation to the people you've identified. There are several ways to do that: phone them, text them, email them, send them a thank-you card, write them a note they'll see when they come in on Monday morning, send flowers, bring a box of chocolates or donuts for the department—whatever you feel comfortable with. The point is, *recognize them*, or—you know what I'm going to say—give them a "hug."

Do this exercise right now, I want you to realize just how simple this process is! At first, the people around you may be shocked by your gesture, especially if you're not known to be "a hugger." Don't panic or be dissuaded. Continue this practice. Persist. Be tenacious. You'll be creating a culture of success. And soon you'll be saying to yourself, "Wow, this is powerful stuff! Why didn't I know about this technique sooner? The people around me are responding so positively and I feel so much better. I'm actually getting a buzz from giving people 'a hug.'"

This tried-and-true technique works. It generates remarkable results without any major investments. In fact, let me suggest very strongly that every business, every organization, should honestly consider, even insist, that all their managers do this exercise as a normal course of managing their people.

The benefits and rewards of regularly offering up acts of recognition, no matter how small, will be to improve productivity, reduce costly turnover, get much closer to achieving people's full working potential, and dramatically improve the all-important and vital bottom-line.

All of that, and more, can be accomplished if paying sincere attention to people is an integral part of the business equation—not in lip-service statements such as, "Our people are our greatest asset," but in real, day-to-day people management practices, such as what I like to call, the "Show 'em" technique:

- "Show 'em" acceptance.
- "Show 'em" validation.
- "Show 'em" appreciation.
- "Show 'em" caring.
- "Show 'em" kindness.

When you're in the "Show 'em" mode of action, your awareness of others is heightened. You become more attuned to saying or doing things that will make others feel better, put a smile on their face, and shower them with well-deserved praise.

"Show 'em" is easy, isn't it? All it takes is a slight turn in the focus you have—from yourself, to the people around you—at work, at home, and at play. No extra effort, no need to take a special course or get special training; just say or do something that recognizes and pays attention to others. Here are some suggestions for you to consider:

Write a thank-you note to someone.

Write a complimentary letter about someone.

Tell restaurant staff they made the dining experience wonderful.

Doodle a happy face and a thank-you on a bill you're paying.

Pay for someone's meal in a restaurant. Tell the staff to tell the people that an angel paid for their meal. Do this at a family-type restaurant and enjoy the reaction and the great feeling it generates. I do that once a week, usually for elderly couples and for those whom I feel will appreciate the gesture.

Here's another real example of how this "Show 'em" thing works. A woman at the Ministry of Transportation helped me with a serious issue. My driver's license had expired and I was about to drive from Naples, Florida, back to Toronto. Driving without a license is very serious stuff.

I was desperate. I called her from Naples and asked for her help. She sent me the renewal license by Express Post—and literally saved me. I could have easily left it at that. But because I'm always in the "Show 'em" mode of action, I wrote her supervisor a special note of thanks and sent her a copy of that letter. Here's the actual letter I wrote:

Dear ABC,

"Above and Beyond"

"Superb Customer Service"

"A Genuine and Caring Individual"

"A Truly Helpful Spirit"

All these expressions, and so many more, describe the incredible service that Ms. J gave me. I wanted you to know that.

She deserves the highest compliment possible because of the help she gave me and the manner in which she was able to resolve my issue. After my initial letter asking for help, she stepped up to the

> *plate with a genuine sense of caring and understanding of the predicament I was in.*
>
> *As my initial letter stated, "I have committed a grave error and I need your help, please." She called me to assure me that she'd be able to help. She followed up with me to provide helpful information. She was reassuring every step of the way.*
>
> *I admit I was very anxious and nervous about what might happen to me. She dispelled that anxiety in a professional and understanding manner. I knew that the matter was in great hands. I wanted you to know that and, through you, to express my heartfelt appreciation and gratitude for the assistance that was provided and the excellent manner in which she handled my grave error.*
>
> *She really earned and deserves every accolade in the book. Thank you very much. And thank you, Ms. J, for saving me.*
>
> *Sincerely,*
> *George Kouri*

Here's the reply I received from her.

> *Awww Mr. Kouri…*
>
> *Thank you so much for your kind words. Wow they really mean a lot. What a great letter to receive on a Friday!*
>
> *Thanks again and kindest regards to you and your family.*
> *Ms. J*

Her response to my email made me feel great. It gave *me* "a hug." And my note took all of two minutes to write. Imagine, just two minutes to add value to someone else's life, to recognize the effort they made, to make them smile, to make them feel good, to make them feel special. Two minutes to accomplish all of that for someone else, in return for which I got the "hug" that made me feel fantastic. Two minutes!

The decision to do anything rests with you. What I can guarantee you is that you, too, will definitely feel a new and rewarding sense of satisfaction when you're in the "Show 'em" mode. I guarantee you'll feel better and get more out of your relationships. Show recognition and appreciation and you'll get recognition and appreciation in return. In other words, you'll get the "hug" you need, too.

And for the sceptics out there, and for those who don't want to believe what I'm saying, here's an interesting quote that appeared in a July 2011 *Fortune* magazine article. It's by Tom Neff, the chief recruiter and senior executive at the renowned Spencer Stuart Company. Mr. Neff says:

> *"The style for running a company is different from what it used to be. Companies don't want dictators, kings, or emperors. Instead of someone who gives orders, they want someone who asks probing questions that encourage the team to think and find the right answers."*

Reinforcing that view is a new survey from Right Management Consultants, a major outplacement firm. It finds that the number-one skill companies seek in managers is, *"the ability to motivate and engage others."*

Those are compelling testimonials, by key people and companies "in the know." They don't use the word, "hug," but they are certainly advocating the same principles we've talked about regarding giving those around you a metaphorical "hug."

3

THE POWER OF RECOGNITION IN THE WORKPLACE

A truly good manager of people knows how important recognition is and makes it an integral part of their management formula. They know that it's not just the bricks and mortar aspects that drive the growth of the enterprise, but rather they appreciate and foster the human elements as well.

And let me be clear, especially for those who think this is a "soft issue." Think about the truly great companies out there. They all share something in common and that is, how highly they regard their people.

The list of the Top 100 Companies to work for is a good starting place for this research. These companies don't just pay lip service to the phrase "People are the greatest asset we have," they actually give life to that expression. They clearly demonstrate respect for their people. They understand the importance of words like dignity, pride, and recognition. And they empower and enable their managers to put the principles of recognition at the forefront of the way they manage their employees.

Here's a quote from the Office of the Auditor General of British Columbia's (Canada) extensive study on *Building a Strong Work Environment*:

> "Recognition has been shown to motivate staff, increase morale, productivity, and employee retention, and decrease stress and absenteeism."

> *"The vast majority of employees who receive recognition or praise feel it motivates them to improve their performance."*

The findings and conclusions of the above study, and others like it, clearly indicate just how vital this matter of "a hug" really is to performance improvement, to employee satisfaction and to a highly productive and profitable business.

Most companies do an annual employee survey to determine the level of satisfaction and engagement of their people. And year after year, the number one need that employees have is recognition. They want the "hug" thing we've been talking about. Check it out with your own Human Resource department.

So, here's a "Dirty Question" to think about: What kind of behavioral modifications is each manager and executive prepared to make to elicit favorable responses in the next Employee Engagement Survey?

Why do I ask the question? Simply because very little is usually done to actually increase employee engagement and satisfaction. I've attended dozens of meetings where the executive/leadership team is convened to review the results of such surveys. They listen while the agency that did the survey goes over the results. A few points of clarification are discussed and then the account executive from the survey company leaves. There's the usual coffee break at this point—and then the discussion really starts.

Here's an excerpt from an executive meeting I attended recently. The President opened the discussion with the expected question:

> *"So, what did you think about the employee survey results?"*

Here's what he heard back.

> *"Well, sir, I'm not so sure about the accuracy of the results. I know in my department, people get along very well. We celebrate birthdays, I send out Christmas cards to everyone, so I don't know why this recognition thing keeps raising its ugly head year after year." (VP Marketing)*

> *How about you (VP Finance)?*

"Let's get serious guys. We're not running a day care center. This warm and fuzzy stuff is not what we should be focused on; we've got more urgent problems to deal with. People have to realize that if we don't focus on generating great results, we're going to be in real serious trouble. This recognition stuff has to be put into its proper perspective, and for me that's not a priority right now."

"How about you? You're the Director of Human Resources, what do you think?"

"Well, I understand where the VP Finance is coming from. We send our people on all kinds of courses to help them develop their skills; we spend a lot of money on training; we have our annual golf outing; we do a Christmas party for employees and their families every year. So I'm not sure what more they want. They have it good here."

Incredible comments! They're real comments from real executives in real companies. Sadly, this is the real world out there in many organizations—not all for sure—but you'd be surprised how many. They miss the point completely.

What their people want is a big "hug"—appreciation, recognition, acceptance, feeling important, and all the other things we've mentioned in that regard—the small everyday acts that make a big difference to employees and inspire them to generate great results. These small acts of recognition are not some expensive program to be introduced and administered and monitored and reported on with stacks of PowerPoint slides.

These everyday acts of recognition are just simple things that managers say and do that reflect human decency and respect for people. They are simple acts that motivate people more than some expensive flavor-of-the-month initiative. Those programs are, for the most part, a total waste of money. They are not what your people want. Period. They want to know that you appreciate them. A simple, personal expression such as, "Thanks for coming in this weekend, you did a great job on that report," is far more powerful than any program you can think of.

And, of course, it has to be mentioned and reinforced that employees do not want to be bullied, intimidated, yelled at, treated like a baby, or put down—or subjected to all the other things that fall under the "Rejection Umbrella."

Managing people is as much an emotional matter as it is a bricks-and-mortar issue. That's the key understanding that is required for effective and profitable people management. Despite that reality, I have yet to bump into an organization that pays a bonus for employee satisfaction. After 35 years of executive coaching, I can't give you one, single, solitary example of a company that does that. Incredible, but true. Not one. Employee satisfaction, which hinges on giving employees recognition, is just not in the bonus or stock-option equation.

Yet amazingly, recognition, in all of its facets, has long been known to be the number-one motivating factor of every normal human being on the face of the earth—regardless of race, color, or creed. Recognition is the key element in building confidence, a key element in building self-esteem and self-reliance. It's the key element in building a person's emotional and psychological foundation.

The benefits of getting into the habit of recognizing and paying attention to others, personally and professionally, are immense:

- You will feel the satisfaction of knowing that you have helped to bring out the best in other people, that you've made a major difference in their life.
- You will have the opportunity to boost someone else's confidence, an exclusive right in the world of work, reserved for those who are in the position of managing other people.
- Helping to build the confidence of others helps you create a lasting, very favorable, and positive legacy.
- Showing your appreciation for other people will absolutely improve the bottom line—guaranteed.
- The ability to inspire, motivate, and build confidence in others is, without a doubt, a major asset to your own personal career—and a very desirable and marketable skill that will give you a definite competitive advantage over others.
- It will certainly differentiate you from others, especially those who think that you have to be a hard-nosed SOB to succeed in business.

- Being good at recognizing others is a highly portable skill that will serve you well wherever you go and whatever you do.
- Showing appreciation also works wonders for raising children and giving them the confidence they will need to manage the many challenges they will face in the real world.
- Equally important, recognizing others will also definitely make you feel great. In fact, you'll feel nourished, fulfilled and—here's the big bonus—you'll feel recognized and appreciated because you recognized and appreciated someone else. Please remember, "Give a hug, get a hug."

Those are significant benefits and it really is up to you to decide to take advantage of them or not.

Here's another point I'd like to stress, especially for those in business. Regardless of what the corporate culture is today, if you manage people, you have the power to do something about giving your people that metaphorical "hug" that we've been talking about—so just do it.

Go ahead and make a positive impact on the people you interact with. You'll discover that it's one of the most rewarding things you can do, and it will help you become a resounding success as a manager. The most significant impact that recognition has in business is that it generates great business metrics, chief of which is a very positive improvement to the bottom line. Indeed, the benefits of active and dynamic recognition are many:

- Helps attract talented people.
- Enables retention of employees.
- Helps develop bench strength in each department.
- Reduces hiring and training costs.
- Results in significant reductions in severance packages.
- Fosters a more efficient and effective operation.
- Inspires people to provide revenue-generating ideas.
- Stimulates a robust execution of growth plans.
- Encourages open communication within the organization.
- Virtually eliminates the fear of evaluation.
- Provides a much healthier and far more positive bottom line.

Excellent managers know the power and the benefits of recognition. They don't take it for granted. They practice its principles on a daily basis and incorporate it into their management style. They fine-tune it as they gain experience with offering recognition. They understand that it's at the foundation of human behavior.

They realize that at their core, people want to achieve. They want to generate good results. They want to please. And the reason they want to do that is that they crave recognition, appreciation, validation, worthiness and all the other good things under the "Recognition Umbrella."

That is foundational. We all grow up wanting to please our parents because we were conditioned that it was the only way to be appreciated, to be hugged, and to be loved. Yet recognition in the workplace is sorely lacking. Perhaps not in every company, but definitely in a huge majority of them.

Here's what I have been told by managers:

"They get paid—they should be happy they have a job."

"I'm not in favor of this soft stuff."

"People have to motivate themselves."

"My job is to bring in the quarterly results—no time for that people stuff."

I could easily fill another few pages with all the excuses, not reasons, I've heard in the past 35 years. But I trust you get the point.

Let's not kid ourselves. A lot of people just don't care about other individuals and this whole thing called "Gimme a hug." You just have to hope you don't work for them, and if you do, brush up your résumé and get the heck out of there. And I say that based on the real examples of exactly what the people I have coached have said and, in many cases, what they've written to me. Here for your consideration are some excerpts from an actual letter I received from an employee in a big, worldwide company. Oh, before I forget, if after you read the note you feel compelled to join this company, email me—georgekouri@sympatico.ca—and I'll put you in touch with them.

I trust this letter, one of many I've received, will help in the understanding of how important recognition really is, and how devastating the consequences of not appreciating your employees can be.

Dear Mr. Kouri,

When I first started working here I really did feel like I was part of a team that respected the contributions that I made. It wasn't always perfect, but there was a camaraderie that we were all in this together.

Sadly this is no longer the case. Service to the client has declined, along with morale. Workplace stress has increased to dangerous levels, tempers are flaring and people have resigned or had to take sick leave due to the strain of working here.

In the past year alone, 16 people have left. That alone, you would think, would make someone at corporate headquarters sit up and take notice, but they keep ignoring it.

I feel as a healthcare professional, that we are viewed by corporate as disposable, necessary evils. In fact, I have over 30 years of experience in this business, yet I am treated like a child by my boss.

I don't want to leave here. I love what I do. I love my patients. I just want to be treated with respect, not put down. The boss has no people skills and that should be addressed by head office.

Really all I want to do is work in an environment that is fair, supportive, encouraging, and one that recognizes the efforts of our people and doesn't make me feel like throwing up every morning. I hope you can help us, Mr. Kouri.

Signed,
ABC

That note was a real shocker. However, what was even more shocking was that the executive team refused to do anything about the situation. One of the vice presidents actually said, "They're just a bunch of complainers at that branch." The president said, "They are lucky to have a job." The VP human resources, who was at the meeting and heard the various testimonials first hand, said absolutely nothing—not a word.

Incredible but true. And here's another shocker: another six people left in the few weeks after this letter was written to me. That's a total of 22 people that left this company in just over a year. It's a perfect example of a "care-less attitude" when it comes to people. Sadly, many companies out there have that exact attitude, even though business history has taught us that companies like this eventually go into the disposal bin, close their doors and sit there wondering, "What happened to our once thriving business?"

I'm sure you can come up with your own answers to that "what happened" question. The fact is there are many managers out there who simply don't get it. Those who do get it and who understand the power of recognition actually make full use of its power and enjoy the immense benefits they derive.

Good managers are instinctively accomplished at recognizing their employees, but the sad truth is that doling out recognition does not come easily to many people. Fortunately, there will be many out there who will read this and give it a try. They'll probably slap their forehead and think, "This is great stuff. I wish I had known about this before." Good on you for being honest and for trying. The most important suggestion I can make to everyone is to give this recognition thing an honest try.

So, how did this fundamental need for recognition, in all of its facets, become so pronounced, and so important? There are many reasons of course—nothing in life is that absolute. However, the one reason that sticks out in my mind and the one I've experienced the most in my coaching business is encapsulated in the phrase I coined years ago:

"People have been taken out of the business equation."

"That's a rather blunt statement, GK. What exactly do you mean by it?"

Okay, maybe I should say that the importance of people has been diminished, perhaps even ignored, or minimized. Pick a phrase or a word that you like. I'll even grant you the argument that it's a generational thing; today's generation doesn't act in the same way that the older generation acted. You're right again. After all, each generation behaves differently than the one before. I've heard all kinds of reasons, excuses, and debates about the statement that "people have been taken out of the equation."

Rationalize all you want. But in my mind, none of these excuses is acceptable, especially when it comes to the way people should be treated. Not a single excuse is okay with me—not a one—and it shouldn't be acceptable to you either.

Why? Because all we do when we accept the myriad of excuses is to tolerate a lower level of mediocrity. That's not acceptable in my mind. All of us have the opportunity to make things better, for ourselves and for the people we work with, even if it's just a bit better. And better is better than the status quo, any day of the week.

The shame is that a lot of people can't be bothered to make things better. They accept what is in front of them. They accept their condition with that infamous line, "It is what it is."

It really saddens me to see so many managers just make excuses for their own lack of desire and initiative to get engaged in the "people thing." They don't realize the vital responsibility they have in managing people. Many just pass the buck to others and to the infamous group called "they" to make things happen.

Sadly, most managers have no idea of the positive impact they can have on others—life-changing impact that helps others reach their full potential. And the most profound realization that many of them don't get is that in helping others, they actually help themselves. Let me repeat that:

"In helping others, you are actually helping yourself."

In any case, maybe we've let "progress" and "convenience" and "faster" and "easier" and all those other words take over our lives, or maybe they just provide us with more excuses for taking people and human contact out of the equation. That results in a major loss for everyone:

- Employees never reach their full working potential.
- Personal confidence cannot be bolstered, just as a flower cannot survive without water.

- Creative ideas and suggestions are scarce because people hold back. Why would they create initiatives when they know they won't be recognized for them?
- The company suffers because instead of having a revenue-generating team, they have a bunch of "9 to 5" employees, ready to leave as soon as they can.
- Poor morale has a direct negative impact on productivity.
- Wheel-spinning is very much in evidence since people have not been given the motivation and respect that drives them to give their best—and this is easily realized when the same topic is discussed meeting after meeting without coming up with a concrete, positive solution.
- The manager shows poor leadership skills by not paying attention to the people and poor leadership is a very costly price exacted on any career.
- It's just not a healthy and dynamic environment that fosters growth and initiative and creativity and, yes, is a fun place to work at.

All of these consequences, and many others, heighten the need for validation, appreciation and all the other items under the "recognition umbrella."

Anyway, by now I'm sure you get the message. Agree or disagree, human interaction has been greatly reduced. No human contact. No thank you. No please. No appreciation. Not a single gesture that even resembles any aspect of the word "recognition." Hence the heightened need for it.

For a lot of people, that's just fine. They like it that way. But if you want to be a better manager, a much better leader, even a much better parent, then please seriously consider, in your own way and in your own style, the tremendous opportunity you have before you.

"*Gimme a Hug*" may well be the greatest improvement opportunity you've ever had for both personal and professional growth—and, incredibly, the easiest to take advantage of.

In the next chapter we'll get into how you can make a proven, but simple, process for recognition a regular, systematic part of your role as manager. By following the eight steps in the next chapter, and practising them regularly, you will become a natural at appreciating others.

4

THE PROCESS OF RECOGNITION

So far, we've talked at some length about just how important and effective recognition can be in the workplace. What I want to repeat here, as an important reminder, is that most people want to achieve. They want to generate good results. They want to please.

That's the starting point and the very essence of this recognition topic. We all grew up wanting to please our parents because we were conditioned that it was the only way to be accepted—the only way to be appreciated—and, yes, the only way to be loved. This pleasing thing becomes life's work. It becomes the prime motivation that drives an individual from one success to the next in their life.

And this desire to please is foundational. Your employees are hoping to be recognized and appreciated for what they are doing. They want to please you, their boss, just as every child wants to please their parents. It may shock you to hear that in your role as a manager you may well have taken over the "parenting" position in a way. Please understand that this is very real and very relevant to the understanding of how to manage people effectively. The fact is, your employees really want to please you, their boss, just as they have always wanted to please their parents.

You need to ask yourself and seriously consider how you are recognizing your employees to help them realize their full potential, just as a parent might consider whether and how they are showing appreciation to their own children.

Think of your employees, your friends, your family, your children, and yes, yourself, and consider these simple truths:

Success Inspires—Failure Hurts
Recognition Builds Confidence—Rejection Destroys It

Knowing this, recognizing others becomes a rather obvious—and powerful—way of managing the relationships you have. Yet this powerful way of managing others does not appear to be top-of-mind for many people. I understand, and I certainly appreciate that. Indeed, it seems to be normal conditioning in the business world: "Get the job done; make sure it's done effectively, efficiently, and make sure it's done right the first time."

Here's what I suggest every manager should also be told:

"Pay attention to your people; part of your responsibility is to bring out the best in your employees. Make sure your people are being recognized for their achievements and contributions to our success, and that your people are satisfied and pleased to work for our organization."

So now let's talk about how exactly we can go about recognizing those who work with us and for us.

Recognition Must Follow Achievement

The first thing we need to do is to understand that recognition is an ongoing process, not an event. Secondly, there has to be a legitimate reason to praise and appreciate someone, or else it has no value whatsoever. In other words, for recognition to be truly meaningful, the individual must first say or do something that warrants recognition.

It is of prime importance for you as a manager to watch out for those moments when members of your team are doing something right or doing something well, and reward them for that. Instead of waiting for them to trip up or screw up so you can tell them what not to do, always try to catch them doing something right and praise them for that. You'll be amazed at the big difference even small acts of such positive reinforcement can make.

Keep an eye out for these "recognition moments." They are priceless opportunities for you not only to have a coaching moment with your employees, but also to make them feel really good and appreciated while learning from, and being coached by, you. And guess what—those recognition moments will almost certainly make you and your employee feel great in the process.

How to Give Others Recognition: A Consistent 8-Step Process

Watching out for recognition moments and taking advantage of them whenever possible is all well and good but, as with most other things on the job, showing appreciation for people on your team will be truly effective and reap tangible benefits only if you follow a proven process that you can apply consistently. Here are some tried-and-true steps in that process that work both professionally and personally.

Eight Effective Steps in the Recognition Process:

Step 1: WHAT to Do—Setting Expectations

Step 2: WHY Do It—Providing Context

Step 3: WHEN to Do It—Time Is of the Essence

Step 4: HOW to Do It—Setting the Parameters

Step 5: Follow Up—Checking In

Step 6: Do It—Leave Them Alone

Step7: Results Achieved—Measuring Up

Step 8: Recognition—Giving That Hug

Step One: "What to Do" or Setting Expectations

The process begins with the "What to Do" aspect. That's the major starting point for virtually everything in our lives.

It is vital that an individual has an objective or goal to accomplish throughout the various stages of their life. It's the way we're conditioned right from the very beginning. We need to know the expectations that others have for us in order to measure whether we've succeeded in our objective or not.

Parents start this conditioning by telling their children WHAT to do and, of course, what not to do. The teacher sets the WHAT to do for students: homework, projects, term papers and, of course, tests, tests and more tests.

The boss tells employees what they have to do. As a manager, you need to set out your expectations as clearly as possible, whether you are asking an employee to accomplish a simple task or something much more complicated. In effect, you are defining what will constitute success or accomplishment, and providing a measuring stick for you and your employee. If he or she achieves the expectations you have communicated at the outset, then that's a recognition moment—an appropriate time to reward that employee for doing the job right, according to what you had both agreed upon.

The fact is that people need to know what is expected of them so that they can "please" their parents, their teachers, their boss, their peers and everyone else in their relationship circle. Think about it. How else can anyone get the appreciation they crave and need in order to thrive? Pleasing others is the answer, and we all learned that growing up. It's foundational. But we'll never know how to please others without knowing what their expectations are.

> *"Got a minute, Jennifer? The big boss is coming in to do his rounds in two weeks. I'll be making a presentation to him and I really want to showcase the great accomplishments of our team. I want you to create a PowerPoint slide show that will absolutely dazzle him and showcase our team members. Take two days and come back to me with a draft. We'll go over it and then you can put your magic touch to it. I'm counting on you and your creative skills. Thanks for doing this."*

That's an example of just how simple it is to set the expectations: "a PowerPoint slide show, dazzle him, showcase our accomplishments, showcase our team, do the draft in two days, we review, then you add your magic touch." And it will take all of a few minutes to set these expectations. Are they clear? Crystal! Now Jennifer knows exactly what to do; she doesn't have to guess, no speculation required, no "left in the dark" thoughts. She can get on it right away and knows how she is going to please her boss. She even got a compliment from him; he thinks she has the "magic touch" when it comes to these presentations.

Jennifer's boss has just created the potential for a "recognition moment," the opportunity to provide praise and appreciation when Jennifer achieves the task he has given her, when she has met the expectations he clearly set out for her. What is vital to note here is that great managers know that they have the responsibility to create these "recognition moments" for their employees. As a bit of a sidebar, it's part of the definition of what constitutes great leadership.

Step Two: "Why Do It" or Providing Context

The next step is the "Why Do It." This is the step that is most often taken for granted. We often make the assumption that people know the WHY, when in fact they probably don't. How could they know what's in the mind of the boss, the teacher, the parent?

Managers talk about "a sense of urgency;" they want quality work; they demand accountability and responsibility; and other such phrases. Yet they don't take the time to explain WHY these things are so important and WHY something has to be done.

"WHY" the objective must be attained should be explained as fully and as clearly as possible, so as to avoid any misunderstanding or confusion. A lot of managers and supervisors are guilty of just "barking" out their orders: "Do this. I want this done now. Just do it and mind your own business." That's not an effective way to manage people or help them learn anything, nor is it an effective way of getting the sense of urgency and the accountability and the responsibility that are vital to success.

The "WHY" explanation should also outline the benefits that will be derived from accomplishing the "What to Do." The WHY explanation is the catalyst that ensures alignment between people; it means that all parties are on the same page. That leads to great work, great teams and that all-important culture of success. The WHY explanation also has the unique built-in benefit of helping everyone in the department, every member of the team, every member of the family, focus and concentrate and work with "purpose" in mind.

It's amazing how much more willing people are to do what's asked of them when they know why they are being asked to do it. Providing context helps them to understand why even the smallest request is important to the bigger picture, and often makes them happier to do something they might otherwise resent doing if they didn't understand the reasoning behind it. Clarity of expectations is vital in the effective management of people. They need to know the "what" and the "why."

In our Jennifer example above, the boss was very clear about the "why"—the big boss was coming in two weeks and her boss was making a presentation to him. Further, he told Jennifer that he wanted to showcase the accomplishments and the members of the team in his talk. That's a very clear "why." It describes the importance of the presentation in simple, easy-to-understand terms. There's no doubt in Jennifer's mind "why" the presentation is crucial and "why" her boss wanted her help.

Step Three: "When to Do It" or Time Is of the Essence

The WHEN to do it, is the next big factor in this process. More often than not, people are told what to do without that vital "when" it has to be done by. That due date should be reviewed and agreed to by both parties—and, of course, respected. Nothing is more annoying for a supervisor than to be told, usually at the last minute, that the activity they expected to be done, won't be done on time—with all the usual feeble excuses.

If more time is needed, legitimately, then the employee needs to have that conversation with the boss as quickly as possible, and an agreement between them must be arrived at. Accommodations can be made when both parties understand the circumstances that have arisen.

In my role as National Sales Director at Ortho Pharmaceuticals, I actually changed the "Due Date" expression to "DO DATE"—"please DO this by Friday at 3:00 p.m., the latest," was what I told my employees. It was a slight variation on the words, but DO implied a sense of urgency that all my people understood—and it helped them focus on what they had to do, and by when.

Knowing what my expectations were motivated them to be prompt and accurate when they submitted things to me. This alignment of expectations really helped everyone on the team accomplish things in a timely manner. And, equally important, it gave me the opportunity to express my appreciation and thanks to them for meeting the DO DATE.

A simple, "Thanks for being on time. That really helps me a lot, so I appreciate your doing that report on time. Have a great weekend." A small act of recognition always generates a positive response. It's a far more effective way of managing people than just taking them for granted. It makes them feel important. They know they've pleased their boss and that's a major confidence-builder. They'll want to do that again and again.

Step Four: "How to Do It" or Setting the Parameters

"HOW TO" do any task should be the responsibility of the employee. They were hired because they had the "how-to" skills to get the job done. By all means, the manager may want to discuss the "how to" with the employee, to ensure they are both aligned, but this is not the time or place to be micro-managing.

Please note that micro-management merely serves to show a lack of confidence in the employee. It questions their ability to get the job done. And frankly, it creates a very negative environment. It's the ultimate hypocrisy in an organization that supposedly promotes empowerment.

Of course, there may be certain requirements the manager has: "Three columns instead of five," "Use the new template sent from head office," "Three lines maximum on each PowerPoint slide." Fine, it's good to outline these requirements. There are always templates that someone at head office believes have to be adhered to. These need to be outlined, explained, and agreed to. Any roadblocks should be discussed and agreed to, as well. Once there is alignment and full understanding of the guidelines, the employee then uses their "how to" skills to get the job done.

A word of caution, please. Many managers choke employee initiative by insisting that things be done their way—the infamous "my way or the highway" style of management. That style should be avoided at all costs. And if you find that you have to explain the "how-to" in detail, then it may well be that you have an employee that is incapable of meeting the needs of the job.

I've never prepared a profit-and-loss (P&L) statement in my career, even though I've reviewed and analyzed hundreds of them. My accounting person prepared them, made sure they were accurate, asked me questions along the way, we had our debates too, and then he applied his knowledge and skills to prepare the P&L and have it on my desk by "Friday at 3:00."

The vital point in this phase of the process is respect for the individual's style, and their way of HOW they would do things and HOW they would execute the details.

The other person may have a different style or a different approach to achieving the objective. They may even have better, more finely tuned skills. They may be more creative, or more experienced in an area of the work. They may even be better than you in a certain aspect of the job. My assistant, Denise, was so much better than me when it came to technology and I'll even admit she was far more creative. It is essential, therefore, that you give your employee the freedom to determine HOW to get the job done. We must remember that there are countless ways of achieving the same objective.

For certain professions, things must be done in a highly exact, prescribed and clearly defined manner. There is little room, if any at all, for individual style. In these cases, it's important to be very clear with each other as to exactly HOW the assignment should be executed. But for many other tasks, individual style, individual methods, and individual ways of doing things are appropriate and, frankly, make the job that much more interesting. For example, I've always done my best work at night. It's currently 3:38 a.m. as I write this section. The point is, my boss didn't give a damn whether I wrote my reports at 3:00 a.m. or at 3:00 p.m.—as long as they met his deadline.

Individual style or approach to how the job gets done is often overlooked by many managers, especially the perfectionists, who think their way is the only way. It's futile to argue with a perfectionist so what I suggest is to take the time to be clear and aligned on all the expectations for the task (what, why, when) so that you can best determine HOW things are to be done. And the way to do that is to ask your boss a bunch of questions, enough to be clear on what is required.

Don't be shy or timid—asking questions shows interest and engagement and bosses love that. Use the "Do you mind if I ask you some questions?" line. It works wonders. I've always used the line, "Do you mind if I ask you a dirty question?" No one has ever said no to me. They're anxious to know what the "dirty question" is. The rule of thumb I suggest goes like this: "Show me your way, boss, or respect my way."

If you are the manager making a request of one of your employees, it is very helpful in this part of the process to add a comment or make a statement that injects the person with confidence.

> "The way you handled the last project tells me you've got what it takes to get this done—and done very well. If you need my help, please let me know. I'm here to support you 24/7."

This seemingly innocent statement is vital in the process. Even before the person starts to work on the task, they know they have the support and help of their manager, no matter how they go about getting the job done. That boosts the individual's confidence and minimizes their fear of failure, which, by the way, is very much at the forefront.

Sadly, this kind of statement is usually missing in action—and because of that, we open the doors to all kinds of misunderstanding and potential conflict. Take a minute to inspire and inject the other person with confidence. You'll be the beneficiary in the end.

Step Five: "Follow Up" or Checking In

The next step is "Follow Up." This is an essential part of the process and it's simple to do: "How are you making out with the report? Do you need any help? If you need anything, please let me know."

All you want to do in this phase is to reassure the person of your support, your encouragement, and your faith in their abilities to get the job done. And, if there are any issues, this step in the process is a good opportunity to get things back on track and set your employee, and yourself, up for success.

Checking in while the task or project is underway demonstrates, in a very easy manner, that you are paying attention to people. Equally important, it takes up little or no time, yet that minute will probably be the difference in getting great quality results versus just the usual "it'll do" kind of work.

The importance of encouragement in this process is easily understood if we think about the example of a baby taking its first steps. The parents hold the child's hands as it stumbles along (support). They say things like, "Come on, sweetheart, you can do it" (encouragement). And after a few minutes they embrace the child and gush with excitement (approval, positive reinforcement), then call their parents and friends to tell them that little Jennifer just took her first steps. Amazingly, the baby doesn't understand the words being used—but they feel and hear the support and the encouragement.

Encourage, support, motivate, and inspire your people. You'll get better results every time—guaranteed. Good leadership requires that the manager provides encouragement while the individual is working to achieve the objective.

Step Six: "Do It" or Leave Them Alone

The next step is the "DO IT" part of the process, leaving your employee alone to actually execute what has to be done, knowing that the now-famous "Friday at 3:00" is the required deadline.

A word of caution, please. This is where the micro-managers rear their ugly heads. They hover over their employees, actually believing that they are helping. The very opposite is true. As I mentioned earlier—and it bears repeating—please understand that micro-management actually promotes fear, the very opposite of confidence. It stifles initiative by the employee: "Why bother trying to be creative? He's just going to change it or do it his way."

Micro-management serves only one purpose, actually two: It hides the true potential of the employee and, secondly, it exposes the insecurity of the manager. Yes, insecurity. Think about that for a minute. All you're doing is exposing just how insecure you really are. It's the same for the yell-and-scream types. The louder they yell, the more insecure they are. So is "insecurity" the perception you want to create by being a micro-manager? If it is, then please understand that true leadership will never be one of your skills.

Please—you've set out your expectations clearly, provided your employee with context for what you're asking them to do, given them a deadline and any required guidelines, and you've even checked in to encourage them and make sure everything is going okay. So for goodness sake, leave them alone now to do the job you have asked them to do.

If you've followed the process laid out here, then you should be very confident that your employee has enough information to do what you've asked of them, and that individual should feel armed for the task with instructions, expectations, support, and that vital injection of confidence.

Having come this far, you've increased the chances that you will both succeed and feel great about the accomplishment. These small acts will have generated a truly dynamic culture of success for your department, and you will have demonstrated great leadership.

Step Seven: "Results Achieved" or Measuring Up

Next is the all-important "Results Achieved" part of the process. The task has been accomplished as requested, and has been handed in by "Friday at 3:00."

If your employee has met the expectations you outlined at the outset, met the deadline, and done good work against the parameters you laid out, then this is the time to take stock of that and reward that person's good work rather than take it all for granted.

It's time for you to acknowledge the accomplishment. You have to indicate that you are pleased with the work the person has done—and they need to know that you are pleased, be that in written form or, even better, by a face-to-face acknowledgment.

Step Eight: "Recognition" or Giving That Hug

All you have to do now is to demonstrate recognition and appreciation. This is the final step in the process and the one that is most often ignored, or overlooked, or taken for granted. When the objective is met, recognition needs to be given. If it isn't given, the entire process breaks down.

And it's extremely simple to express, even if you're not in the habit of opening the "umbrella of recognition." Here are some examples:

"Great job on that report, Henry."

"You're a genius, Louise, that presentation was very creative."
"Thanks, Jennifer. That helps me quite a bit. My boss was very impressed. I really appreciate the work you did."

"Thanks for coming in on the weekend. That shows dedication and I thank you for that."

Simple, small statements that will make a big difference to your people.

Here are some other suggestions. Forget email as a way of expressing your appreciation. Make your thanks special by doing it in person, by writing a short note, or giving the person a thank-you card. Recognition has more importance when it's done in these ways as opposed to the "thx" that I see so often—and that drives me crazy. The individual has spent the last week or more working their butt off and all they merit is a "thx"? Let's get real here.

Always make your acts of recognition special and important, no matter how small or easy they may be. Give them weight. It's only going to take a minute to do that, yet the resultant benefit to you and to the individual will be huge.

One of the most important facts to remember about recognition is that people will not ask for it—recognition must be given. That's the way we have all been conditioned—as children, as students, as employees. The fact is, we all do things to please others because we hope to be appreciated by someone else. When that recognition comes, we're motivated to do it again because we want the appreciation once more. We become "recognition addicts."

However, if recognition is not forthcoming for a job well done, then we back off; we might withdraw, give up, do the minimum, just get by, and all those other negative states and attitudes. Think about it—why would anyone like their job when they are never appreciated for what they do? And by the way, it's never about money.

The above process is straightforward. It works. It generates excellent results and enables you to manage people better—at work and at home—effectively, efficiently and with great results and great satisfaction. And the best part is that the how-to methods are simple, easy-to-use, and can be implemented immediately. Let me repeat some of the key benefits we've been talking about:

- Recognition is a powerful motivator.
- It's a prime confidence-builder.
- It's the fuel that drives people to achieve great things.
- It creates a positive working environment.
- It builds and strengthens the morale of the team.
- It gives people the opportunity to reach their full potential.
- It creates real business success.
- It fosters and creates incredible people success.
- It's a superb demonstration of great leadership.
- It leads to a higher level of personal satisfaction.

Recognition Is a Vital Process

I cannot leave this section without relating a true story to prove just how important the working environment is and how vital the process of recognition is to people.

Several years ago, I was flying to a meeting with Don, the vice-chairman of a major consumer products company. This man was in charge of all the subsidiaries outside of the USA. He had a corporate jet at his disposal, made huge dollars, lived in a mansion, and had all the trappings you'd expect an individual of his stature and power to have.

During our conversation I asked him, "My understanding is that you started off in the mailroom and here you are in charge of most of the world. How did you do it? What drove you to such an incredible achievement?" Without hesitation he replied, *"Two things: insecurity and people.*

> *"I've always had to prove myself as far back as I can remember. My feeling of insecurity was a constant force that drove me to prove that I was good enough. I wanted my father to be proud of me. Insecurity became the "WHY" I did things and my major motivation. Because of my feeling of insecurity, I was always trying to prove myself to others.*

> "Work was a great way of showing others that I was good enough. I figured out that as long as I was getting great results, the company would never get rid of me. No one fires good people who get things done. In fact, they kept promoting me and giving me new responsibilities. The recognition they gave me drove me to continually achieve good results.
>
> "I also recognized, early on in my career, that it's the people in a company who get things done. I was just the conductor of the orchestra; they played the instruments, they made the music. I was just conducting.
>
> "Therefore, it made sense to me that if you treated people with respect and in the way you would have liked to be treated, you'd reap big dividends and have a more positive working environment. So that's what I did throughout my career in all the positions I had—and here I am today."

The point is that work enabled Don to prove that he was good enough, in the eyes of others and in the eyes of his father, who, indeed, was extremely proud of his son and what he had achieved in his life. He was also very proud that his son never forgot his humble beginnings and always treated people with respect, or as he told his son, "Do unto others ...."

Don's insecurity and his passion to please others drove him to achieve. His sensitivity to the importance of people enabled him to create a positive working environment. He treated everyone, at every level of the company, with respect, with courtesy, and gave them the recognition and appreciation they had earned. In other words, he gave them a "hug." As a result, he become a huge success. And he did it by sticking to a simple formula that he believed in:

Create a Positive Working Environment

Treat People with Respect

Don became my best friend. He passed on a few years back. I still miss him terribly. He was a great leader and a great human being. God rest his soul.

It's not like that for everyone, but it's important for managers to recognize that work, for many, is their primary source of esteem, confidence, and importance. Work validates their worth as a human being.

Again, no one will ask for recognition; you have to give it. We've already shown the disastrous consequences of not giving appreciation to others for the good work that they do and, even worse, of making them feel rejected in any way.

However, if you follow this simple, proven, eight-step process for incorporating recognition into the daily life of your company and your team, you'll be surprised at how easily you can instill a culture of success and accomplishment. Make recognition a habit and a business process and you and your employees will reap the incredibly positive and rewarding results you're guaranteed to achieve.

5

EASY WAYS TO GIVE OTHERS RECOGNITION

The power of recognition is absolutely awesome. That is because you can have a tremendous positive impact on another person's life. The impact you make can last a lifetime.

Remember the high school teachers that you loved so much? I bet you can talk about them for hours, with a smile on your face and a tone of appreciation for the influence they had on you.

We've all heard the statement "the best boss I ever worked for," haven't we? In fact, most people can refer to an individual they consider to be just that, "the best."

We all seem to have fond memories of various people who made a positive impact on our life. And when you think about it, what did they really do to have such a powerful influence on us?

The ones who gave me a "hug" I remember with great fondness and deep respect. I am so grateful to them for the attention, recognition, and teachings they gave me. I miss all of them. It truly is a lifetime of wonderful memories. Recognition like that is very powerful, and yet it can be given in very small, very easy, and very simple ways.

Okay, so what can you do—especially given the immense time pressures that most managers have—and given the fact that the topic of people management is often not #1 on their list of priorities?

Put People Back on Your Agenda

The first thing I'd like you to do is literally put people back on your agenda. Try this technique: actually write "People" at the top of every day in your smartphone or other calendar. Do that for a few months and look at it every day to remind yourself that the people you work with are a top priority. The reason I'm suggesting you do that is that the reality of business today is that we tend to take the people around us and the people who report to us for granted.

Committing in writing to making people a priority in your workday will help you in making recognition a habit. You'll be amazed at the results you'll get and the sense of satisfaction you and your employees will start to feel. You just might earn a spot in that "best boss I ever had" category.

Boost Confidence

When a person achieves their objective and is recognized for it, their confidence has no choice but to increase. But it will not go up by itself; someone else has to recognize the accomplishment and be pleased by it—and express that pleasure to the individual. A child needs to hear that she has pleased her parents. She needs to hear the words and feel the emotions associated with having pleased them. The same holds true for a player on a team—he needs to know that the coach is pleased with his play. At work, employees need to know that their boss is pleased with their performance as well as the efforts they're putting in to achieve the desired results.

The human condition is such that we need others in our lives; we need to share our successes, and our failures, with others. That's the essential point. It is only when the recognition and appreciation come from others—parents, teachers, coaches, bosses, friends—that we truly feel confident, accomplished, worthy, valuable, important, and so on.

Recognition from others is the best confidence booster. And with an increase in confidence, the individual is ready to tackle the next objective. In other words, they are motivated to do it again.

Here's a great tip you can start using right now. Ask yourself:

"What can I say or do to boost someone's confidence today?"

Please indulge me another comment. If you're not used to giving praise and appreciation, which a lot of people find difficult to do, I understand. I understand, because the fact is that it is difficult to give appreciation when you yourself are in need of it. I've coached hundreds of people in that category. They certainly had the technical skills to become a manager, a senior executive, even the CEO of the company, but they found it very difficult to get into the "hug" business. They just couldn't bring themselves to give praise and recognition—until they learned and understood the techniques we're talking about here.

Most of them were amazed at the reactions they experienced, and, more importantly, the incredible self-satisfaction they derived from showing appreciation to others. Giving hugs and getting them in return helped fill some of that emptiness they had carried with them for decades.

It may well be that you were not showered with praise and recognition as you were growing up, but please remember that today, right now in fact, you have the opportunity to go out and get that recognition and appreciation—by first giving it to someone else and getting it back immediately. Don't lose that opportunity.

The "Shoebox" Principle: Write Thank-You Cards

Many people I know have an old shoebox where they keep special cards and letters they've received from other people. From time to time, they sit back and read them and reflect on all the great memories these cards and letters generate. It makes them feel good.

My wife, Marlene, still has and still reads a letter of appreciation she received from Mrs. Estée Lauder 40 years ago, handwritten and signed by Mrs. Lauder herself, not some PR person. It meant so much to Marlene to get that letter. Today, 40 years later, it still brings back fond memories and still makes Marlene feel great.

Here's an interesting story for you. I came home one day to find Marlene crying like a baby. She had Mrs. Lauder's letter in her hands. I asked what was going on. That day, Mrs. Lauder had passed away and Marlene wanted to read that special letter and say a prayer. We both sat there and prayed and cried. It proves how powerful this thing called personal recognition really is and how much of an impact it has on an individual, even 40 years later.

I advocate and strongly suggest to all the people I coach and all the audiences I speak to, that they write cards and letters to the people they manage and the people in their personal circle. And I do that because people do keep handwritten cards and letters. They have much greater meaning than an email, especially those that spell "thanks" as "thx." Email notes don't make it to the shoebox.

So now some "Dirty Questions," and you need to be honest with your answers:

- How many cards or letters of appreciation have you written and sent out lately?
- How many cards or letters have you received during your career?
- How did you feel when you got them?
- If you have never received a note of thanks and appreciation, how does that make you feel?

Here's a helpful hint: Write the word "letter" in your calendar in the first time slot Monday morning and the last time slot on Friday afternoon—and do that for the next few months. Now write two letters of appreciation and send them out. It's a great way to start and end your week. I guarantee it will make you feel great. Remember—"Give a hug, get a hug."

Another helpful hint: Please don't use email. In fact, I beg you not to even think of email for recognition purposes. It does not have the same importance as a handwritten note or a personally signed card. It just won't be perceived as being all that special. Writing a personal note will take only a few minutes to do, yet its impact can last for 40 years, or more. Here are some examples of quick notes that will make a tremendous impact.

> *Dear A, I just wanted to tell you how much I appreciate your efforts on Project X. I know you spent a lot of time on it and I'm grateful to you for doing that. Keep up the good work.*

> *Dear B, I know it took extra time to complete the report I asked you for regarding X. The information you provided is vital to me. Thanks for the extra effort. It's very much appreciated.*

Dear C, I'm sure you were disappointed in not getting the contract/order for X but I want you to know how much I appreciate the work you put into it. Your presentation was excellent and the data you provided was top-notch. You gave it your best shot and that's what I value. Thank you for doing that.

Dear D, Last Thursday I left my office at 9:00 p.m. and noticed that you were still working away in yours. Just wanted you to know that I appreciate all the extra time you're putting in these days. Thanks a lot.

I can't think of a single human being who wouldn't be delighted to receive any of the above letters from their boss. They're short. They take less than a minute to write. And you can bet your last dollar that they will have a very positive impact on the person receiving them. I also hope you've noticed that it wasn't just the "big win" that was being recognized in these letters. It was the extra time and the extra effort. That's a very effective way to motivate and inspire people.

The reality of business is that not every proposal will be accepted. It is far more important for the long-term success of the organization to recognize the effort put in and thus encourage the person to go on to the next project. In other words, take the opportunity to motivate them and build their confidence as they move forward.

Recognition, in its various dimensions, should not be just for success stories. The encouragement, acknowledgment, approval, and reassurance aspects of recognition are essential elements that build confidence and motivate people to take new initiatives and create new ideas for the betterment of the organization.

And I want you to put all of that in writing because it means so much more to the recipient. Go out today and buy a bunch of thank-you cards. Every Monday and every Friday, write a note to someone in your own department or to someone in another department who has been helpful to you: "Jerry, just wanted you to know that, once again, you and your team came through for us with those extra cases. It really is amazing how helpful that was. You have a great team so please express my gratitude to all of them."

Writing a thank-you card will take about 60 seconds to do. That's not a lot of time to show appreciation and recognize someone.

Meetings

You probably spend countless hours attending meetings. What a glorious opportunity to express appreciation to people.

Recognizing someone publicly for a job well done or for a great effort can have an even more positive effect than a private thank-you. Recognizing an employee in front of his or her peers and perhaps other managers can be incredibly rewarding and confidence-boosting for that person. It costs nothing, and can be hugely effective. So before you go to a meeting, think of one or two people who deserve recognition for their efforts—and express that at the meeting.

This public appreciation will not only have a positive impact on the people you're thanking, but it will also reflect extremely well on you and your leadership. You'll gain the respect of others for such an act of public recognition and you'll be a role model to others, showing them how to appreciate others by your actions.

The Positives Review

Another great way to create a positive and appreciative tone at meetings is to begin each meeting with what I like to call a "Positives Review." Simply take five minutes at the start of every meeting that you convene to recognize and pay tribute to the achievements or efforts that people have made in the last week, or the last month, or the last quarter.

I say that because most meetings I've attended start off with the usual business review, which ends up being a litany of all the things that went wrong or didn't happen: "We missed the forecast by 6 percent. Such and such a retailer ordered much less than they originally said they would take. The competition pulled a fast one on us and, frankly, ate our lunch." Those situations may all be true, but I cannot urge you enough to stay away from starting any meeting in that manner. It sets a negative tone and shuts down the conversation, as well as the all-vital "solution-providing" part of the meeting (ever notice that the same topic keeps coming up, meeting after meeting, without resolution?).

Instead, start every meeting with a Positives Review. Look for success stories, for special efforts that people or departments have put forth; pay tribute to an idea that was generated by someone, to a particular sale or event that was successful. This can be recognition of an individual, the entire team, or even the whole company. It's amazing how many good things you'll find when you start to look for them.

That review of the good stuff sets a positive tone to the meeting and encourages people to participate more actively in the discussion. This short "Positives Review" creates a powerful impact on everyone and makes meetings a pleasure to attend.

Schedule Positives-Only Meetings

Another suggestion is to convene a meeting once a quarter with all your direct reports just to review the success stories and achievements of the quarter. To repeat, forget the usual business review agenda. This special meeting is to discuss only what your people did well and how they did it.

Acknowledge the creativity that was demonstrated, the above-and-beyond efforts that were put forth, the ideas that you got, the initiatives that people took, the successes they had, successes that other departments had, the fact that there were no back-orders, that such and such a retailer doubled their order of the promotional item—any and all positives that each member of the team put forth during the quarter.

A word of caution. Since people aren't used to this sort of thing, the first meeting will probably be fraught with scepticism as they all wonder, "What's going on here?" Just tell them that you're delighted with the positive things they have done and that you wanted to take time to talk about those achievements. It's your opportunity to give them the recognition they need. You can also follow up the meeting with a note to everyone to thank them for their achievements.

The techniques above are some very simple ways of showing appreciation, paying attention, and recognizing people. They don't take much time to execute. Over the course of a few months, you'll have created a very positive environment, one where people feel recognized and appreciated. You'll be well on your way to creating a culture of success—all because you responded to every "recognition moment."

6

STOP REJECTING, START COACHING

Now that we've spent time looking at the power of recognition, the benefits of openly appreciating others, and exactly how we can go about doing that on a regular basis, it's time for a reality check.

Let's face it, not every act is worthy of recognition. People will make mistakes. We inevitably will have to deal with our children, colleagues, direct reports, and others dropping the ball, making an honest error, or completely screwing up. The important thing is how we choose to deal with those mistakes.

Just as we learned to look for "recognition moments" to train ourselves to look for something positive to praise—so too we must learn how to turn mistakes into "coaching moments"—moments that turn a negative event into a positive learning experience for the person, rather than making the individual feel hurt and rejected.

Here are two examples of dealing with a minor mistake:

> "The presentation you made this morning was awful. It was totally off-message. All it did was prove that you really don't know what you're talking about. You were a major embarrassment to our department."

That approach is pure rejection. It hurts. It reprimands the individual. Learning cannot take place. It's a lost opportunity for the manager.

This next example takes advantage of the opportunity for the manager to coach his employee. Rejection is not necessary. With coaching, the employee will learn and be encouraged to make the necessary modifications to improve.

> *"You and I need to go over the presentation you made this morning. You made some good points, Henry, but there are some key areas I'd like to review with you so that we make further improvements for the next presentation you'll be making next quarter."*

Before we get into the "coaching moment" concept, I want to open the umbrella of rejection and take a look at exactly what's in it.

Rejection manifests itself in various forms: scolding, reprimanding, bullying, intimidation, threatening, verbal or physical abuse, yelling and screaming at another person, a hand gesture of dismissal, the middle finger raising its ugly self, a look of disgust, shaking the head in rebuke, a harsh tone of voice, and, of course, angry expressions and foul language.

The umbrella also contains subtle and not-so-subtle forms of rejection: ignoring the other person, refusing to talk to the other person, walking right by someone you know but not saying anything, the deadly silent treatment, and so on.

The point to note is that rejection of any kind hurts. Some forms of rejection are more painful than others, some more extreme than others, and some have a life-long negative impact on others. I want to reinforce the point that some forms of rejection can damage a person for life. That's why I'm hopeful that people will realize how much of an impact they have on others and how damaging rejection, in all of its forms, is to other people.

In the normal daily routines of a workplace, it's just not necessary to hurt another human being. It's unproductive. It debilitates. It affects the productivity and the profitability of an organization. It has absolutely no useful purpose, not a one. Rejection is destructive. Let's get into an example to further amplify this vital topic.

Consider the following situation. The sales person just notified his manager that he did not get the order he told his boss he would get. As a result, the division would not attain the targets they had promised—not a good situation to be in for any business, especially when rule #1 is, "make a commitment, deliver the commitment."

Obviously, the sales shortfall issue has to be dealt with. It's not something any manager should ignore, especially because it can be a valuable coaching moment. The question is *how* to deal with it.

First, let's realize that the manager will be angry, probably very angry, because the sales target has not been met. Moreover, he will have to answer a lot of questions from his boss; he has to come to grips with the fact that it's his failure as much as it is the sales person's; and he has to realize that his leadership may be questioned. He doesn't look good, and failure doesn't please anyone. So he's likely to do what so many people normally do in these situations: blast the person who made the mistake. That may well be the accepted and "normal" way of dealing with mistakes in some organizations, or according to some people. But we all know that getting blasted is very painful and debilitating.

The other major consideration is, who is going to fix the problem? The person who made the mistake or the boss? If the boss fixes it, as many do, then they are abdicating their leadership role. If the employee is going to fix the problem, as they should, then they need to be in a frame of mind that enables them to fix the problem, that encourages them to learn from their mistake and develop a plan, or modify their behavior, to ensure they will not repeat the error.

What needs to be remembered here is that put-downs are a painful form of rejection and therefore the individual will not be in any mood to work, let alone fix things, if they are made to feel rejected and hurt.

The reaction of the employee really depends on how the boss responds to the individual when the mistake is discovered. In that regard, please consider the following two approaches.

> "I can't believe that you screwed up so badly, Jerry. We went over that a thousand times. I told you how important that was, and yet you dropped the ball and now we'll never hit our target. How the heck did you let that happen? It's totally dumb. Now get the hell out of my office. I have to clean up the mess you created."

> OR...

"Jerry, we have to talk. Two weeks ago you assured me that retailer X would order the cases that would enable us to meet our target. They didn't come through and now we're not going to hit the forecast for the quarter. That's very disappointing, to me and to the entire department. So I have to ask you, what happened and how did it happen? How do you want to manage the situation at this point? What were the lessons from this incident? What new initiatives and actions will you take to prevent this from happening again?"

It should be obvious that the latter approach is generally more effective in the management of people. The boss has certainly expressed his disappointment with the mistake, which is important to do. It's essential that people know when mistakes have been made so that they can learn from them.

The difference between the two approaches is that the disappointment has not been personalized ("totally dumb"), nor does it contain explosive language ("get the hell out of my office"). Personal attacks hurt. They are pure forms of rejection. The person being attacked has no choice but to withdraw and retreat. They cannot be in an inspired mood, ready to find a solution and create an action plan. Moreover, the more constructive approach generates some additional benefits:

- It compels Jerry to think about alternate solutions to the problem and, in doing so, he becomes far more committed to solving the matter than when he was kicked out of the office.
- It will ensure that Jerry learns from the incident, since he has to think about what happened and why it happened. Even more crucial, he has to come up with an action plan to ensure it doesn't happen again. It forces reflection on his part and does so in a more positive way than being scolded, as in the first approach.

I can't emphasize enough that people can't think straight when they are being reprimanded, threatened or intimidated. They just can't. Unfortunately, many managers and supervisors just blast away and yell and scream at the person who's made the error. It's somewhat understandable when one considers the conditioning we all seem to have: "Mistake Made, Blast Away." But is that the most effective way of dealing with the mistake made, or the most effective way of managing people? The tragedy is that the opportunity to teach the person who made the mistake is forever lost; nothing positive emerges from the incident, no learning takes place.

After all, instead of the boss and the employee working together to resolve the issue and take corrective actions, the rejection of being blasted by the boss silences any creative solutions and inhibits any behavior modifications in the future.

A key point needs to be made here. Not all forms of rejection are the "blast away" type. Rejection does not always come in such extreme forms. Most people won't get overly angry or abusive in the workplace, or at home for that matter. Rejection can be much more subtle but still just as hurtful and debilitating. Indeed, many managers choose not to deal with the mistake made. They sweep it under the rug and, in doing so, retreat from the mistake-maker. They don't talk to him. They might ignore him, not engage him, and just "put up with him." Even more subtle is when any form of recognition becomes absent from a manager's feedback. In those cases, the employee doesn't feel bad about being scolded about a particular incident, he or she just simply never gets the chance to feel good by being recognized, resulting in comments such as, "I've never heard a thank-you in my 22 years here."

We Are Conditioned to Notice the Negative

The fact is we are naturally wired to notice the mistakes that people make rather than exactly the opposite. That helps to explain why turning recognition into a reflex is not easy for most people. Unfortunately, we are better conditioned to focus on negatives rather than on positives. And if you don't believe me, please look at your local newspaper, or watch TV, and see if you can find a positive story. Turn on your radio and listen to the "shock-jocks" and tell me what is positive about them. That's our conditioning. We're conditioned to seek out the negative over the positive, the mistakes rather than the achievements, and then to take out the guns of rejection and "let 'em have it."

Kids get time-outs, they're told to go to their room, they're told no to this and no to that, they're grounded, and so on and so on. In the business world, rejection manifests itself via remarks as diverse as, "That's going to lower your bonus, Jerry," "I hope you understand that your mistake will be reflected in the rating on your performance review," "Forget the luncheon we had planned for next week," and many more.

I'm amazed at how creative people get when it comes to the various dimensions and forms of rejection they dish out—and how much time they spend rejecting others. And then they tell me, "I don't have time for that recognition stuff." By now, we have seen the damaging effects of rejection, of focusing on the negatives and on the mistakes, to the exclusion of positive recognition.

The Damaging Effects of Relentless Rejection

Rejection is hated.

Rejection is a major negative force.

Rejection hurts—it hurts like hell.

Rejection is not something anyone wants or enjoys.

Rejection is a prime destructive force.

Rejection destroys people.

Rejection destroys relationships of all kinds.

Rejection destroys confidence.

Rejection inhibits initiatives.

Rejection drives people to depression and hopelessness.

Rejection drives people to say and do bad things—some very bad things.

The reality of work, and of life, is that people will make mistakes. Individuals fail at one thing or another. Everyone knows that failure is to be frowned upon. In business, serious mistakes are usually recorded in the individual's file and then noted in their annual performance review. That has a negative impact on their rating and thus on their compensation and on their bonus. The mistake-maker has to pay for his or her transgressions.

If enough mistakes are made, then the consequences are far more disastrous, usually resulting in the employee being dismissed.

The point is that most people accept the notion that mistakes and failures are punishable, and that there has to be some form of "payment" exacted on the mistake-maker. I understand this rationalization, but I just don't buy it nor do I accept it as a standard for the way mistakes should be handled and the way people should be treated when they make them. Sorry, but I just don't buy these so-called reasons, nor should you. What I do buy, so to speak, and what I'm trying to advocate here, is that our conditioning can be modified; that we have an opportunity to make things better, and to treat people better when mistakes are made.

My view and my recommendation is that rejection should be tempered as much as possible—minimized, if you will—and not dished out in extreme formats. I'd love to say that rejection should be eliminated from the human lexicon, but that is not realistic. Decades of conditioning to see mistakes and focus on the negatives are not about to be reversed by me. I wish I could, but what I hope to achieve, at least, is to get through to a bunch of people and open their eyes to the debilitating impact of rejection in all its various forms, and perhaps get them to modify their behavior.

Perhaps the work done by Dr. Guy Winch will also help to achieve that objective. Dr. Winch has done extensive research on the subject of rejection and writes about its impact in his book, *Emotional First Aid*. Here are some direct quotes from his book, which will help put this topic into perspective and, I hope, assist you in better managing the people you come in contact with.

> *"Rejection is such a strong emotion that the body actually registers the sensation as if it were a physical pain."*
> *"Rejection is distinct from other negative emotions because of the magnitude of the pain the feeling emits. In addition, feeling rejected often elicits a whole host of other negative emotions."*
>
> *"Rejections can cause four distinct psychological wounds. Specifically, rejections elicit emotional pain so sharp it affects our thinking, floods us with anger, erodes our confidence and self-esteem, and destabilizes our fundamental feeling of belonging."*

Dr. Winch's book contains very powerful findings on the topic of rejection. If you're a manager of people, it should be on your must-read list.

The conclusion about this topic of rejection should be very clear by now: it's very painful; it's debilitating; it shuts people down and is a very destructive force. Most people accept that and say, "That's just the way it is." I simply cannot accept that. I believe that we all have an opportunity to make things better, and I truly believe that we have a responsibility to try to make as many things better as we can.

So, how can we make this rejection thing better? Can the conditioning be modified? Yes, it can, very definitely! But let me make this important distinction. The objective is not to change the individual or their psychological make-up. That's a futile exercise that is virtually impossible to achieve. However, behavior and conditioning can be modified. People can learn new techniques of saying and doing things. They can learn new ways of managing various situations. New behavioral techniques are constantly being created and new formulas being developed. Once exposed to these techniques, an individual's behavior can be modified. The only catch is that the person has to be motivated enough to want to make things better and try new methods. Let's be clear about the objective and the how-to.

Modify Behavior? YES
Change the Person? NO

Modifying the individual's behavior is the key and in that regard, it is important to remember the following points:

- The human condition is such that people will make mistakes. To expect otherwise is folly, although perfectionists tend to drive themselves silly striving for perfection.
- Some mistakes are within the control of the individual, many others are not. That is an important aspect when it comes to modifying the person's behavior.
- Some mistakes are minor, others are major, some are catastrophic. All these categories have to be recognized and given their rightful due.

- A mistake, however defined, usually has to be fixed, and, as obvious as it may sound, the fixing has to be done by someone. That's what all mistakes have in common. People have to make it right. That has to be taken into consideration as behavior is being modified. Specifically, is the person in a state of mind to rectify the situation or have they been rendered ineffective?
- Modifying behavior often requires that difficult, even negative, feedback has to be delivered. How that feedback is delivered is a crucial factor in determining whether or not the individual's behavior will be modified.

Let's move on to the vital topic of how to turn a negative—the mistake—into a positive behavioral modification. In other words, how we can turn a mistake into a coaching moment, rather than a rejection.

7

HOW TO MANAGE MISTAKES

Mistakes are inevitable, but a purely negative reaction to them that causes the person who made the mistake to feel the pain of rejection is not. Varying circumstances demand varying reactions. But in every circumstance, it's important to learn how to turn the mistake into a coaching moment. Following are a few methods that can be applied immediately.

Step 1: Classify Mistakes

Realize that not all mistakes warrant the same reaction, so learn and adopt the practice of classifying mistakes and then apply the kind of reaction that's appropriate to that classification. For example:

- No reaction (1)
- Mild reaction (2)
- Medium reaction (3)
- Hot reaction (4)
- Very hot reaction (5)

Use a 1 to 5 scale if you prefer to use numbers. The key benefit of this technique is that it gets you to realize that not all screw-ups warrant the same outburst from you.

On a personal level, for example, if you catch your spouse in bed with another person, that would qualify for a "very hot reaction." If your child spills a glass of milk, that probably calls for "no reaction" or "mild reaction." If you realize that BlackBerry shares are at $8.00, when you bought 2,000 shares at $150 each, then go ahead and blow your top off. If one of your employees is bullying another person, then you should have a "very hot reaction," a (5) on the scale; but if they are five minutes late with the report you requested, give them at most a (2), a "mild reaction" on the scale.

The important point is to realize that not all mistakes warrant the same reaction, so classifying them may help you better manage your reactions and the potential damage you're likely to inflict on others.

Here's a true story that may help to illustrate what I mean. One of my clients was proud to tell me that he locked his two-year-old son in his room for half a day because he had dropped a glass on the kitchen floor. You be the judge. Is that reaction (a 5 on the scale) warranted? If your answer is yes, then let me quickly and strongly suggest that you need to take an anger management course—immediately. Locking up a child in their room for hours is an over-reaction to this situation. It will damage the child for the rest of his life. That's why it is so vital for every parent to understand that that kind of abuse, yes it is abuse, will leave a major scar on that individual—for life. Moreover, please understand that they will not get over it. They can't. Nor will they be able to forgive and forget. They can't do that either. It's impossible. They will carry that "Hurt File" (more on that term in Chapter 10) with them to their grave—and they'll always remember that you were the culprit. What a legacy to leave your child.

It's the same at work. We all remember the bad bosses we had. We can still recall the verbal onslaught we had to endure, or the poor performance rating they gave us, how they yelled at us, and how they embarrassed the heck out of us in public. I often hear that it's very difficult to control emotions when mistakes are made. That may well be the case, but let me remind everyone that we have already learned how to control our emotions, and we do it consistently and we do it very well. The fact is, most people have a great ability to control their reactions. They do it all the time. Here's the proof:

- How is it that you don't yell and scream when you're talking or negotiating with a customer? You may be thinking he's a

miserable so-and-so, but you control yourself and don't tell him that, do you?
- How is it that we are able to control our temper when we're talking to the president of the company we work for? We may be thinking, "He's tough and arrogant," but we'd never say that to him, would we?
- How is it that we don't punch the dentist in the mouth when he hurts us with that root canal stuff he's doing?
- How is it that you wouldn't dare swear in front of clergy?

I've been tempted to call some people certain names. I'm sure you have too. But the fact is, we've learned how to control our anger, control our language, and control our actions, even when we've been hurt, or rejected. We've all done it. So adopt that same approach as you classify the mistakes and the emotional stuff that's happening around you.

Step 2: Be Tough on Issues, Not on People

Learn to differentiate between the issues and the people involved. Adopt the practice of being tough on issues—very tough on issues—but respectful of people. There are two reasons for this. I want you to become a true leader, one who knows what he wants and inspires his people to achieve success. Second, the person you may be yelling at and putting down is probably the same person who will have to fix the issue.

How can they possibly do that when they've just been chastised and torn to shreds? If you scold them, intimidate them, perhaps even abuse them, then you diminish their confidence, if not destroy it completely. And then if you tell them to "fix the damn problem, or else," how effective do you really think they will be? How does your behavior inspire the other person to fix anything, or to act in an efficient and effective manner? It is far more effective to manage the issue without putting the individual down, without berating them or being nasty to them. Turn the situation into a positive "coaching moment."

- Be demanding, very demanding, on getting great results.
- Insist on generating high performance.

- Be relentless in getting your people to meet expectations.
- Use definitive language, "I want this done" (just add a "please").
- Be insistent that people meet deadlines, "This has to be on my desk by Friday at 3:00 p.m."

Go ahead, be tough on issues, but not on the person who made the mistake or whose performance has not met your expectations. Here's a process that will help you discuss what happened with the individual responsible for the mistake, without the need to berate them:

- Find out what happened. Why did it happen?
- Discuss and understand the consequences of the problem.
- Ensure that the person knows this is unacceptable.
- Let the person explain his version of the matter.
- Clearly state that greater attention and focus are imperative.
- Tell the individual that they must be more disciplined in their approach.
- Insist that deadlines be respected and met.
- Outline the "musts" that are essential to the success of the business.
- Demand that the individual prepare an action plan to avoid repeating the problem.
- Ensure you are both aligned with the action plan.
- Agree to a follow-up meeting to ensure execution of the plan.

If you focus only on putting down the individual and exacting some sort of punishment, you won't succeed in changing the other person's behavior; you'll succeed only in alienating them and causing them to shut down because they feel rejected. Here's a more specific example of what I mean:

> *"It's been two weeks since we talked about getting that report. Are your ears blocked or are you just plain lazy? Your attitude is terrible. I really don't appreciate it and you're reaching the point where you and I have to have a more difficult discussion. I'm really fed up with your attitude."*

I hope you notice that these comments are only about the individual, not a word about the issue and why it is so important; why it has delayed progress; the significance of being on time with the report; and why it is important for the business. And what about the next steps to correct the situation and move the business forward? There really is no need to berate, or intimidate, or abuse the employee to get the point across and get the issue resolved, which ultimately has to be done.

When you think "coaching moment," the focus is on making things better; on improving the way things are done; on modifying the behavior of the individual; on learning new techniques; on developing new skills; on how to be more effective and more efficient; and on improving the working environment.

The other reason I suggest being tough on issues rather than on the people is what that approach says about you and the perception it creates about you. When you yell and scream and intimidate others you're simply demonstrating just how insecure you really are. You're waving the flag of insecurity for all to see. The rule is simple: the more negative you are, and the louder you scream, the more insecure you are. As much as you might disagree with that assessment, it is an unassailable fact. Just think back to the Negative Nellies, and the yellers and screamers you've encountered, and come to your own conclusion. I want you to become a great leader—not a negative so-and-so.

Step 3: Don't Punish, Coach

This is a new concept for most people, especially because our conditioning is to seek out the mistakes, the failures and the poor performance of others, and then to exact revenge, to get even, don't let them get away with it—punish them. I certainly understand that it's not always possible to turn a negative into a positive. That's being realistic. But what I want to reinforce is that in order to be a better manager and a much better leader, we need to give serious attention to the great opportunity to make things better for ourselves and for the people we interact with.

Within the heart of every mistake, every failure, every poor performance, I believe there lies "a coaching moment." Great leadership seeks out that coaching moment and maximizes the opportunity it gives to make things better. Great leaders know the value of coaching, even though we have been conditioned to reprimand and punish.

We've all graduated from the PP School—the Picky Picky School of finding mistakes, of finding failure, of finding poor performance in others, and of finding the negatives of life rather than focusing on all the positives that exist. I scratch my bald head and ask myself—WHY?

- WHY is punishing easier than praising?
- WHY is punishing more acceptable than praising?
- WHY is punishing viewed as strength, yet praising is wimpy?
- Why is there time to punish—no time to write a thank-you card?

What a shame that people actually think and behave that way. What I recommend is, don't punish mistakes, instead choose to use the opportunity to coach and, therefore, improve the situation.

Don't Punish, Coach

So how exactly do you turn a mistake into a coaching moment? Let's use some examples to show the difference between negative feedback that hurts and rejects the person who made the mistake, and constructive criticism that can help to fix the mistake or avoid it in the future, and that will certainly make the person who made the mistake feel better about moving ahead with a positive attitude.

In this example, let's assume that Jerry was asked to make a presentation and it went badly. His talk was too long, disorganized, and his supporting slides were ineffective. It was embarrassing for the audience to watch, and for Jerry himself; he knew he was struggling in front of the audience. The first scenario is that Jerry's boss gives in to his knee-jerk reaction to blast Jerry for not doing a good job with his presentation:

> "It was stupid of you to make so many slides, Jerry. I don't understand what you were trying to prove. No one was impressed; they couldn't even read the slides because you had too many words on them. And the charts you did were terrible, too complicated, and made without regard to the audience. What a total waste of time."

This negative feedback focuses on the mistakes, offers no assistance with coming up with a solution or advice to improve in the future, and is hurtful into the bargain.

Every manager is faced with situations like this—a mistake, error, poor performance, a screw-up of some kind on the part of an employee. Here's an approach to consider using instead. First of all, call the individual into your office—have a private discussion, never do it in public. Next, instead of simply blasting the employee for what went wrong, ask some probing questions to get to the bottom of what really happened:

- So, Jerry, tell me what happened, and why you think it happened.
- Okay, are there any other possible explanations?
- As you look back on the matter, how would you approach it differently?
- What would you have done differently with your slides?
- What did you learn from the incident?
- I want you to create a plan that will incorporate the lessons from this so that your next presentation will be spectacular.

Here's a very different script than the one in the first example above, more of a coaching script than a "blasting script."

> "Jerry, one of the things to consider when you're working on your presentation is to first write out any and all of your thoughts on the subject. A brain-dump often helps to get you focused on your speech. Then go over those thoughts and organize them in the most important order. You're a good organizer and you should use that skill. Then look over what you've written down and ask yourself if that's the key message you want to convey to the audience. Notice that I said 'key message,' not the kitchen sink and everything in it. The best speeches are those that have focus and a singular message, obviously supported with two or three facts. We have to remember that the retention level of any audience is limited; you started off okay but then got into so many details that the audience was turned off and tuned out. At a certain point they just didn't hear a single word, and the shame of

it is that I know you worked very hard to get all those PowerPoint slides done. And that, by the way, is another aspect I want you to pay attention to: fewer slides, fewer words on each slide, and stick to the key message. Are you good with that?"

Perhaps the "Don't Punish, Coach" concept is a novel approach for you. That's fine. And I agree that not every incident may fit the bill. But I still want to encourage you to give it serious consideration because it will help you make things better and it will help you become a better leader. Imagine the feeling of power you'll have, actually turning a mistake into a coaching moment that helps build the confidence and experience of the other person.

It really is a glorious feeling. I want you to experience that sense of satisfaction. So, please, consider and try the "Don't Punish, Coach" technique. It's a major departure from what we are conditioned to think and do. Yet it is one of the most positive and most satisfying techniques to use in managing people.

> **Punishing:** Providing negative feedback, berating, bullying, and so on, only serves to shut people down. It stifles progress and the possibility of making things better, making things more efficient, more effective.
>
> **Coaching:** Lifts people up. It adds to their skills bank for life, opens the doors to personal and professional growth and all kinds of positive progress, improvements, and a much easier and fulfilling life. It helps in reaching a person's full potential.

The "Don't Punish, Coach" Process

First, recognize that a mistake has been made. The boss and the employee need to do this as soon as it happens. Do not delay dealing with the matter, be it an error, poor performance, or one of those "crazy mistakes." Putting it off to another time serves no purpose because you will lose the coaching moment. And if you ignore the matter, it may be interpreted as condoning the mistake, or that you are too weak to deal with the matter. That's a label you'll wear for a long time and, as a manager, you need to avoid any sign of weakness. Deal with the issue immediately.

As a sidebar, one of the main reasons people put off dealing with a situation is that they want to avoid what they see as conflict; one person has to point out a discrepancy or an indiscretion to the other person, and for many that is just too uncomfortable to do. So they put it off until another time, "I'll talk to him when he's in a good mood," "I don't want to upset him now," or they forget about it all together.

In my view, dealing with the issue is not conflict. I see it as giving the other person a gift, yes, a gift. Think about it. If you help someone get better, improve their skills, or teach them a new how-to, you are giving that person a gift. And that gift may last a lifetime and help them immensely in their career and in their personal life. It's not conflict at all, unless you blast away at the individual and put them down. My first boss, Tony, taught me so much about selling and customer satisfaction that I can never repay him for the insights and techniques he showed me—and they have been with me for decades. Peter, my other boss, was a walking encyclopedia in business, and his coaching moments with me have served me very well in my coaching business. I appreciate the moments of so-called conflict we had; I'm a better person because of them. So thanks, Tony and Peter, for all of your coaching.

The second part of this process, although it has to happen as soon as you discover that an error has been made, is to do whatever it takes to keep yourself silent and under control. Accept that your immediate reaction may be to vent, to react negatively, or even to explode. Remember that you are more than capable of controlling your emotions and have proven that so many times—remind yourself that you never explode at the priest, a customer, the dentist, and so on.

Now I understand that there are situations that will cause you to explode. Fine, but remember what we said earlier in this chapter—classify mistakes and thus classify the degree of your reaction. And regardless of where you score on the scale, try to remain calm and measured. That's the sign of a great leader and a great boss. Take a moment to regain your composure if you have to, and then shift your brain into the "coaching moment" opportunity. You're going to coach rather than punish. And you're going to do that because coaching is the gateway to knowledge, to learning, to personal and professional growth. And, to repeat, because coaching, rather than blaming, makes you a much better leader and a much better boss.

Now use your skills and knowledge to coach and help the other person learn from the situation that just happened, be it an error or poor performance. Remember, the key thought you need to condition yourself to have is that your discussion with the individual is not about reprimand or scolding—we're staying away from that approach. This coaching moment has everything to do with helping the other person develop and grow and, in so doing, with giving them a lifetime gift. Let me share some general guidelines that will help you do this with great satisfaction.

After you've acknowledged the mistake, screw-up, or performance issue, then try to find something, anything, positive in the situation and point that out before analyzing and correcting what went wrong. Focusing on the positive out of the gate, even for a moment or on something small, will help to put the employee in the right frame of mind, will let him know you're not going to blast him for the error, and will make him much more receptive to the constructive criticism you have to offer.

In the example above, the manager pointed out early in his feedback that Jerry is a good organizer and that he can apply that skill to the problem at hand. Later in the discussion, he returns to focusing on the positive in acknowledging the amount of hard work that Jerry did to prepare his slides, even though they could have been done better. Don't you think hearing those positive comments makes Jerry more ready to accept his boss's advice on how to improve his slides and his presentation overall?

Focusing on something positive in the situation can be helpful to set the tone for any coaching moment, but the number-one principle for coaching discussions is to get the person talking and to ask as many questions as needed to keep them talking. I say that because you should know what's in his or her head rather than making assumptions about their behavior or the thoughts behind it. You want to know how much thinking they've done before, during, and after the situation happened. It's important for you to get his or her perspective. Armed with facts, you can then coach the individual from a much better position.

Asking questions and keeping the doors of communication open will tell you what skill set the individual has; what his capabilities are in this area of the business; does he have what it takes to do this job, or is he in over his head? Equally important, you want to see how seriously he takes the matter. What's his sense of urgency to remedy the matter? Does he show creative thinking? Is he a solution provider?

All of this information, and more, comes out by your asking 1,001 questions—and listening to the answers. Key to this part of the process is that your role is twofold: ask questions and listen. Do not judge what he's saying. Managers get themselves into debates and true conflict because they start to argue with the other person; they disagree with what he's said; they want to pontificate about how they would have addressed the matter to prove that they are smart, and so on. Button your lip and listen to what he's saying. That's the only way you're going to learn about the person sitting in front of you. And that knowledge will guide your actions with this person in the future.

Obviously we can't cover every possible situation, but here are some questions that will help to guide you in these coaching moments. Please feel free to modify them to fit your exact circumstances and the person you're talking to.

> *"So Jerry, we both know that what happened is not good news. It hurts our department. It has a negative impact on the results that we wanted to achieve. How do you want to respond to this matter and get things turned around?"*

> *"Mary, let's take a few minutes; I want you to tell me exactly what happened. What transpired that led to this situation blowing up?"*

> *"Thanks for telling me that. Can you please elaborate on that point? I want to appreciate what the customer's position is. Did he offer any other alternatives or suggestions for managing this in the future?"*

> *"Let me ask you a 'dirty question,' Barry. How do you want to manage this issue? How do you think you can make it right? How do you see us addressing this shortfall with the other members of the team and with the executive board? I need to have your plan of action no later than 3:00 p.m. on Friday."*

> *"I hear you Steve, but I'm not sure it completes the picture. Fill it out for me. It's just not the Steve that won last year's award. Can you help me understand what's going on with you? Because it's the only way I can help you; it's the only way we can both move forward."*

Please notice that there isn't a single word that comes close to scolding or bullying or reprimand—not a word. Yet the messages are clear: this is not a good thing, it's going to upset the team, what happened, why did it happen, what's going on with you, you need to resolve this matter, need a plan of action, need it urgently, willing to help you.

The technique is to keep the person you're coaching talking; the more information you get the better. In other words, I want the ball in his court. As tempting as it may be, as the manager/supervisor/parent, you must avoid becoming a "doer" and taking on the responsibility of fixing the matter yourself, even though you may know how to do it with your eyes closed. You must maintain your leadership position. And it is vital that your employee fix the issue because in the process they will learn—and that is the ultimate objective. Of course you can add the statement, "If you need my help, please come see me." The mistake maker, the poor performer must resolve things if they are to develop and grow—and you need to give them that opportunity. The coaching technique demonstrates powerful leadership:

- It demonstrates strength of character on your part.
- It shows your willingness to support and encourage the person who made the mistake because you haven't blasted away.
- It teaches you a lot about your employee and his or her thinking, abilities, and skills. Your 1,001 questions will draw this out from them.
- It helps clarify your relationship with the individual and helps you better manage the person.
- It fosters a culture that allows mistakes to be made, so long as learning and personal growth are the result.

- It helps you to maintain the individual's dignity, rather than create a "Hurt File," which we will talk about in detail later on.

You may not have used the 1,001 questions technique before. Not to worry—it works, so prepare for it, and practise it. And remember, make no judgment of what your employee says, just listen attentively. At all times, I want you to maintain and enhance your leadership position. Do not resort to being one who berates people because they are having a bad hair day. I want you to advance your career and become a superb leader. You do not want to create the perception that you are a bully, which leads us into the next chapter.

8

ZERO TOLERANCE FOR BULLIES

Here's one of my "dirty questions" that provokes much thought and debate when I ask it:

"If people are your greatest asset, how come you tolerate employees being bullied, yelled at, screamed at, and being psychologically abused?"

That question pops up quite often, especially when I'm called in to deal with an abusive situation or a dysfunctional team in a company.

The answers I've heard from senior management are beyond surprising. In fact, it's shocking just how much this kind of bullying behavior is tolerated, even condoned, in the business world. What's even more shocking to me is that most organizations do not see it as "bullying." To them it's just being "a hard-nosed, tough manager," and, of course, to them, that's perfectly acceptable. For example, here's an actual, direct quote from the President of a very large organization:

"X is such a brilliant executive—so what if he loses it once in a while? What's the big deal?"

Well, it is a very big deal, because of the negative impact it has on the financial health of the company and because of the human toll it exacts. If people are the greatest asset, then organizations need to ensure that their employees are being managed in a respectful manner. There should be no place for bullies—zero tolerance.

That sounds like the right thing to do but, amazingly, it just doesn't happen as it should. Bullying is tolerated. Many actually believe that it's part of business to yell and scream at others and to put people down. One of the chief reasons for this is that in so many organizations, technical skills always trump the people management skills. The fact is that many bullies in the business world are very competent in the technical aspects of their job. However, their ability to manage people is lacking, sorely lacking. Many of them just don't know any better. And yes, some are too entrenched in their ways and have developed a "don't care" attitude when it comes to other people.

They yell and scream. They intimidate anyone and everyone. They can only be classified as bullies. And sadly they rationalize their behavior with a simple, "That's just the way I am." That may sound okay to some ears, but in my experience, the bullies can be far more effective and more fulfilled when they learn new ways of managing people; when they learn how to recognize and appreciate them rather than hurt and reject them.

The fact of the matter is that people are not as engaged or productive in an environment that is negative, or abusive, or full of put-downs. It's that simple. In the workplace, a negative environment is a big deal because there is a big financial loss. Let me prove that by doing some number crunching. For the purpose of this exercise, let's assume there are 100 people in a company, working at a 70 percent efficiency/effectiveness level. That's clearly a loss factor of 30 percent. Now the simple math:

---

100 people working a 40-hour week
4,000 hours of work each and every week
At an average of $50 per hour =
$200,000 per week

If the loss factor is 30%,
We're losing $60,000 per week
52 weeks per year – less 2 weeks' vacation =
A loss of $3,000,000 per year

$3,000,000 per year down the drain

Unbelievable, but a fact. A hard fact that should make every CEO wonder, "What is going on in this company?"

The loss factor is real, it's tangible. It's real money taken away from the profits of the company. That has a negative impact on the organization's ability to invest in the growth of the business. Equally vital to realize is the heavy toll it takes on the well-being of the employees and on their productivity levels. Here are excerpts from an article written by Sue Shellenbarger in the August 15, 2012 *Wall Street Journal*:

> *"No one forgets a screamer—a boss who yells at workers, leaving them feeling powerless and constantly on edge, and sometimes reduced to tears when the explosion comes.... 'Yelling is a vestige of a past time.'*
>
> *"Indeed, the yelling boss appears to be quietly disappearing from the workplace. The new consensus among managers is that yelling alarms people, drives them away rather than inspiring them, and hurts the quality of their work."*

You can't escape the fact that where there is bullying, the impact on productivity and profits is negative. The "loss factor" is huge, all because people have been bullied in one way or another.

Coaching Bullies to Control Their Behavior

Modify Behaviour?   YES
Change the Person?   NO

Years of coaching others has confirmed for me that people's behavior can be modified and that people can control their behavior. In the case of bullies, dealing with them is more challenging and it does take more time, but it can be very successful. Here's an actual example that demonstrates that.

I was once asked to work with an individual who was just returning from a six-month sick-leave. I asked the human resource manager what she expected me to do with this person. Her reply was, "We suspect he's been bullied for a long time by his supervisor, Mr. A, and finally couldn't take it anymore. So we want you to find out what really happened and then recommend a course of action that we should take."

I was tempted to say, "Just punch the bully in the nose and then fire him," but I refrained. First, I had to find out the facts and, if verified and accurate, I would apply my knowledge and experience to try to get to the root cause of why Mr. A bullies people and see if there is a course of action to help him dramatically improve his behavior. And, given a few months of coaching, if he was not capable of modifying his behavior and adopting new techniques, then we may have to take a different course of action, and you know what that is.

After doing a lot of homework, and asking 1,001 questions, I learned that he had a reputation of being a "straight-shooter," so that's exactly how I was going to approach him; he was direct with others, I was going to be direct with him. My first question to him was, "You know why I'm here, so how can I help you?"

He wanted to change, but didn't know how. I listened carefully as he talked for almost an hour. I guess he wanted to get it all out. When he stopped, I decided to ask him a very "dirty question":

"Is bullying your pattern of behavior at home, and could it be that it's the main reason your first wife left you?"

The silence in the room was deafening. It was a very "dirty question," some might even consider it too dirty. But I was coaching an individual who had reached out to me for help and whom I believed was truly a brilliant individual, whose track record of success in business was impeccable. However, his people skills were questionable.

In this "help me" state of mind, there was no time to waste. I had to dramatically move him to a more "people focused" style of management, one that validates the individuals around him, rather than putting them down, and that included his personal life as well as his work life, which my research had validated.

So despite the long silence, and some tears, and reflective moments, he finally stood up and thanked me for being so straight with him. We had several more sessions and I'm thrilled to say that, yes, he's a much better manager now and a much better father and husband. His bullying is under control.

There are some realities that need to be understood when dealing with bullies:

- Most bullies don't realize that they are bullying others. They've yelled and screamed at others all their life, so to them it's "normal" behavior.
- Bullies aren't born—they are created. They are created by not being appreciated, by being put down, and by being made to feel "small" throughout their childhood.
- So the individual's quest to feel important, to feel worthy, to be appreciated and to stop feeling small, takes on a new dimension and a direction that can only be described as negative. The individual goes about making himself feel bigger by making others around them feel smaller. The idea behind it is, "if I put you down, then I'm bigger."
- Putting other people down makes the bully feel very powerful. They inject others with a large dose of fear. This gives the bully a large dose of strength, more than they had growing up:

  "I'm a 'somebody.' They fear me. I'm strong. I'm tough. I am important because everyone around me is afraid of me. I tower over everyone. I'm big."

  While this may seem like a warped sense of feeling bigger and more confident, it's very real and it satisfies the bully's need to be accepted, to feel important.

Yes, that's a simple explanation, but it serves the purpose of expanding our knowledge of how bullies are created—and how we can help them modify and control their behavior.

In the workplace, most managers simply don't know how to deal with the bullies they have on staff. Certainly there was no indication that they were bullies when they were first hired, primarily because the focus was on their technical skills, most likely not on their interpersonal skills.

There is a huge warehouse of anger, frustration and stress in the head and heart of a bully. They are in constant pain, and they just don't know what to do to free themselves from all the hurt that has built up over the years. Put in other words, they are in a prison they don't know how to get out of. What they do know and what their mode of operation has been for so many years, is that they make themselves feel bigger and more important by abusing others. They haven't learned that, or been shown how, one of the ways to be recognized and appreciated is by lifting others up rather than putting them down.

At the heart of the various techniques that will help the bully is that he has to learn to say and do positive things that will lift others up and make them feel appreciated rather than put down, and that will, in turn, make him feel appreciated, important, validated, and all those other feelings under the "Recognition Umbrella."

All we can realistically hope for is to help the bully control their behavior in the workplace. And I say that because the scars of an abusive childhood just can't be erased. It must be made clear to them that abusive behavior is unacceptable. It's zero tolerance. If control is not a possibility for the individual, then they probably should be dismissed. Having described those realities, the question remains: how should we go about dealing with a bully? Here are some thoughts for your consideration.

Pay closer attention to his or her accomplishments: make a list of the technical skills he has, the achievements he has made in the past six months, the positive things he's said and done, and the positive impact he's had on others in the organization. Armed with this list, convene a meeting with the person. That meeting has two objectives: to review the positive aspects of this person's performance, and to point out that he has, indeed, made a positive impact on various people—they appreciate him, they think he's great in various aspects of the job, he's looked up to when it comes to the numerous technical skills he has. "Maybe these other people haven't expressed their appreciation directly to you, but they sure have mentioned how good you are to me as your manager. That's one reason I wanted to talk to you today. So how does that make you feel?"

His response has to be positive; this type of feedback makes him feel very good, appreciated, and validated. In other words, all the good stuff he's been trying to get all his life.

> *"I'm glad you said it makes you feel appreciated because that's the truth. You're a valuable member of our team, but I have to be very open and candid with you and ask you a 'dirty question.' Are you okay with my asking you that question?"*
>
> *"How are you going to modify your behavior and stop making the people around you feel so small, even bringing some to tears? How can they possibly think you're a good boss when you drive them to tears by what you say and how you treat them? How can you possibly get the acceptance that you yourself want so badly?"*

These are tough questions to ask but they have to be asked. Please note that a bully really believes he is all-powerful, that he is feared, that no one around him has the guts to stand up to him. These questions do just that and thus throw him off his game—he's been found out.

He's going to react, he'll be very defensive about his actions and his behavior toward others. He'll come up with a thousand excuses. Fine, just let him talk, let him vent because he knows that you've found him out. And please don't use the "bully" word in your discussion.

Then get into exactly what you want him to do—no time in this situation for 1,001 questions. His strategy and tactics to date have been to bully others and put them down. He doesn't know how to make himself feel good or important any other way. So, as his manager, you can help him by giving him some very clear direction and techniques.

> *"You've proven you have the ability to please some very important people in our company because of the good things you've accomplished. You've obtained acceptance and appreciation from them because of your positive actions and your technical abilities. So I know that you can do what I want you to do from this moment onward."*

1. *I want you to stop putting your people down immediately. I don't care what mistakes they're making or what it is that upsets you—just stop putting them down. I do not want to hear about people in tears in your department—period. Here's what I want you to do.*

2. *I want you to make a list of the positives each of your employees has—their skills, their accomplishments over the past six months, how helpful they have been to their teammates and to you. Get that done by Friday at 3:00 p.m. and we'll review it together on Monday morning at 9:00 a.m.*

3. *Then I want you to call a meeting of all your people—hold it in the boardroom next Friday—and review the list of positives you've made for each person. And yes, do that in front of everyone. I want the entire team to realize just how good you see them to be and how appreciative you are of them and their contributions to our success.*

4. *I want you to follow up that meeting by writing each person a personal "thank-you" letter, handwritten by you, and given to each of them in person. In fact, print the "positives list" for each person on nice paper and get it framed, then give that to them within a week after the meeting.*

5. *On the last day of each month, I want you to hold a "stand-up" meeting in your office to review all your team's accomplishments for the month. It will enable you to express your thanks to them, and lift them up in just 15 minutes.*

6. *After your stand-up meeting, we will get together and talk about your team and review how things are going and how you're feeling about this new method of managing your people.*

7. *I also want you to think about other things you can do to enhance how others—your team and even other departments—perceive you and your management style.*

8. *After you've done this for two months, I want us to meet for a few hours and go over how you'll be able to take advantage of what I'm going to call the "coaching moments" that come up from time to time. And just so you know where I'm coming from, I'm well aware that mistakes will happen, but rather than call them mistakes I prefer to call them coaching moments. We'll go over how to manage in that mode rather than in the blaming mode.*

9. *All of this will make you a superb leader and get you out of the pattern of putting other people down. You've got great technical skills. I want you to become a more complete manager who combines great technical skills with great people management skills. That's what I want for you.*

I hope you notice that nothing in the above sounds like reprimand, or anger, or put-down. You have to be in a helping mode when you do this and your tone of voice has to be helpful as well. If you're not in that helping mode, you will sound just like his parents sounded decades earlier—and that's a death sentence to this technique. He'll relive those painful moments his parents put him through and won't listen or absorb a single word you say.

Yes, it's a challenging process but it can be very successful, because the individual sees you as helping him become better; he sees you as someone who accepts him, who appreciates him, rather than as someone who puts him down.

The process above can generate good results in the modification of the bully's behavior. You don't have to be a psychologist to do it. As I said earlier, just get yourself into the helping mode and approach your discussion with that mode in mind. You're helping the individual, not reprimanding him.

And, frankly, if the individual is incapable of modifying his behavior, at least be comforted by the knowledge that you tried to help him. And then proceed to remove him from his position. In such extreme cases, do that for the sake of the other people on the team, and for the sake of the business. Your efforts to create a culture of success and to be a great leader will not be realized with bullies around.

9

ESTABLISH A NO-BULLIES POLICY

Yes, it's possible and here's the proof. In my 15 years at Johnson & Johnson, in various positions and various departments, I never heard a put-down, never witnessed any kind of abusive behavior, never saw anyone crying in their office because their boss just ripped them to shreds. None of that behavior ever took place.

It was a corporate principle that everyone understood and was pleased to adhere to. It was in the Johnson & Johnson Credo. That's how they wanted the company to run and how they wanted everyone to behave. In fact, one of the first things you did when you got a job was to read and understand the Credo—and agree to abide by it. It made working enjoyable, productive and, yes, profitable.

Here's a true story I want to share with you to prove that a "No Bullies" policy can be very productive and very successful for the company and for its people. My former boss, Peter, just called to invite my wife, Marlene, and me to dinner with his wife—that's 35 years later. It was like we've never been apart. My boss taught me a lot. He truly cared about me. He encouraged me. He let my creative spirit flourish, and most important of all, he allowed me to be myself and to use the skills I had. We accomplished so much together. That's powerful stuff. That's proof positive that people working together can achieve great things when the environment is positive, productive and harassment-free.

Despite what many think, you don't have to yell and scream to get things done. You don't have to put people down to achieve success. My boss never yelled at me, ever. He encouraged me—he gave me "a hug"—and when we finally saw each other a few weeks ago, it was even a physical one.

I mention all of this because he accomplished all of his immense success from the ground up, starting his career as a sales representative and making it to CEO of one of the world's largest health-care companies. He did all that through hard work and determination and personal sacrifice, without berating, or yelling at, or abusing, or bullying people. In my language and from my perspective, he knew how to manage people and how to apply the principles of "Gimme a Hug."

- He was clear about his expectations.
- He had a keen sense for revenue-generating activities.
- He had vision and an acute ability to know what the priorities were.
- He set high performance standards for the department.
- He was demanding and was always there to support your efforts.
- When errors were made, learning, rather than punishment, took place.
- He allowed people to use their skills, talents, and creativity.
- He never micro-managed and never raised his voice at anyone.
- He was a superb communicator.
- When the objectives were met, he made it his business to recognize the people who achieved them.

He was, and still is, a truly great leader and a very special and wonderful individual. Indeed, this example demonstrates how senior management can use its power and authority to outline clearly what it wants done and how it wants people to act and behave toward each other.

I understand the quarter-by-quarter chase that business is in; the vital need to meet the EPS (earnings per share) estimates; the competitive challenges that have to be faced; the time pressures; the number crunching; and all the other demands and sacrifices that have to be made. As one of my clients put it, "It ain't easy in here." I understand all that. I was part of that world. But what Tony, Peter, and Don taught me is that you can deliver great results and create a culture of success by first understanding that it's the people who make it happen and therefore that they should be treated with respect and given that metaphorical "hug"—and never bullied.

True leaders can set the rules, the expectations and the how-to right from the start. Please consider the following guidelines as an example of how you might create a credo for your own company.

> *"We at ABC Inc. do not tolerate bullying or abuse of any kind. We do not tolerate putting people down, degrading them, intimidating them, or any demeaning behavior. Any such actions are grounds for immediate dismissal."*

The Company:

We foster and promote a positive working environment.

We provide a working environment free of harassment and bullying.

We insist on people being treated with respect and dignity.

We care about our people and demonstrate it in real terms.

We promote a team spirit approach at all levels of the organization.

We insist on open communication without fear of reprisal.

We will endeavour to bring out the best in our people.

We want our people to be proud to say they work here.

We insist on high performance at every level of the company.

We will recognize and pay tribute to results achieved.

The Manager:

My manager treats me with respect and dignity.

My manager makes me feel important.

My manager values and appreciates me.

> My manager is genuinely concerned about me.
>
> My manager takes the time to recognize and praise my efforts.
>
> My manager is trustworthy.
>
> My manager is a good coach and mentor.
>
> My manager is a great listener.
>
> My manager welcomes my ideas and suggestions.
>
> My manager communicates his/her expectations very clearly.
>
> My manager is very helpful and encouraging.
>
> My manager expects high performance.

Feel free to modify these lists. Having guidelines and standards regarding the human element of business is good for the company and great for its people. And it has a positive impact on the bottom line.

Please allow me to mention some other facts for those who are having difficulty accepting all this stuff about bullies and the way people deserve to be treated. First, I'm sure everyone will agree with the following statements.

- Satisfied employees will perform to their capacity and thus show a good return on investment. From the historic Hawthorne studies conducted in the 1940s to the present day, it has been proven that workers who are satisfied, delighted, happy (pick a word) in their job are more effective, more efficient, and more productive. That has a positive impact on the bottom line.
- Dissatisfied employees will not perform at their peak levels. Poor performance leads to waste, mistakes, sabotage, spinning wheels, and other negative actions, all of which have a negative impact on the bottom line.
- A "No-Bullies Policy" is not a warm and fuzzy issue. It's real. It's tangible. If bullying is tolerated on the job, real dollars are being taken away from the profits of the company and, sadly, the well-being of every employee in the company suffers.

- You can't escape the fact that there are real business costs to bullying behavior and its negative consequences.

Cost Factors

The tremendous cost of fixing the mistakes made

The loss of customers because of poor service

The shutdown and re-start costs on a production line

The theft and sabotage that goes on

The cost of turnover and severance packages

The recruiting process, which involves ads and countless hours of interviews, agency fees and other items

The cost of training and development to bring new employees up to par

---

All of these costs, direct or indirect, take away from the profits of the company. That's a lot of money. Wasted. And despite all the rationalization that takes place to cover up the costs of ineffective people management, the fact is that all of these cost factors can be greatly reduced, if not completely eliminated, by paying attention to people and giving them the "hug" they cry out for in survey after survey on employee satisfaction.

Turning a Bully Around: From Intimidation to Collaboration

Confronting a bully takes courage, especially if you're an employee or a colleague rather than that person's boss. But having the gumption to face a bully and call him or her out on that unacceptable behavior can be a powerful tactic. Here's a story that illustrates how understanding and support from a colleague helped to turn a bully around—how the antagonist became the ally.

The desperation in her voice was rather shocking. I guess that's one of the reasons people come to me for coaching. They need help and so I was pleased to listen to what Liz had to say.

She was having major problems with one of her colleagues. He was creating all kinds of conflict between her team and his team: yelling and screaming at meetings, intimidating her people, playing the "it was my idea" game, and always acting like the big shot who knew everything. He was an insecure bully—in fact, all bullies are insecure.

I suggested to Liz that she had to confront him and let him know his behavior was unacceptable and damaging, not only to her and her team, but also to the growth and progress of the business itself. I told her I'd give her a few how-to tips on how to manage the conversation.

Standing up to a bully is not an easy thing to do, especially since most people hate what seems like, feels like, smells like conflict. They're afraid to confront people like this for fear of being slapped down, for fear of being made to feel small, and for fear of the intimidation and invective being turned on them. But here's what I told Liz:

> *"The bully has already rejected you through his intimidation tactics, his berating, his playing politics, his yell-and-scream attacks, and so on. All of these actions are not actions of acceptance; no matter how you look at it, they are pure rejection."*

> *"You've already been rejected by the bully and, if I may point out, rejection by any other name is still rejection. So what are you worried about? What have you got to lose? The person has already rejected you."*

So what do we do to confront someone like this? Here's a note I wrote to Liz on how to handle the matter.

> *What I want you to do is to let him know that you will no longer tolerate being bullied or intimidated by him. Tell him, "I know your game, but I ain't playing it." It's not easy to do because we're not conditioned to confront these bullies, but confront him you must, or he'll continue to intimidate you and your people, and your people will see you as a weak manager. Is that what you really want? You've told me, "I can't do this." I hear you, but I can't accept that. It's not a matter of "I can't;" it's a matter of how-to. Let me repeat that: It's not a matter of "I can't;" it's a matter of how-to.*

So let's go through this step by step. Frankly, you'll surprise him, and even shock him out of his bully boots. Here's a suggested flow and some talking points for your discussion.

1. Thanks for agreeing to meet face-to-face.

2. The reason I wanted to meet you is that I want us to have a positive and productive working relationship, which, if we are both honest about it, has not necessarily been the case in the past few months. Whatever the circumstances were, whatever the reasons were, whatever the details were, I'm sure you'll agree that it has not been a very motivating and inspiring atmosphere for either of us.

3. We now have the opportunity to move forward and create a far more positive environment for ourselves and for all the people on our teams. It makes good sense and it makes for good business. And with the recent acquisition, we both want our people to be firing on all cylinders—and you and I need to be fully engaged in building and growing our new business together.

4. If I may assume that you agree with all of this, the next question is, how do we achieve this? How do we go about strengthening our working relationship? How do we ensure that our people and our company benefit from this new and positive environment? Here are some thoughts, suggestions, and ideas, for your consideration.

5. Let's not clean our dirty laundry in public. We both know that challenging issues come up from time to time, so suggestion one is that you and I meet privately, face-to-face, or talk to each other on the phone to manage the issue. Email should be avoided on these tough issues because it's hard to write and capture feelings and emotions via email.

6. Let's keep the temperature cool between us. There's no need to flare up and get nasty with hurtful comments that berate and

> demean people. Yelling and screaming hurts—it hurts badly. It destroys any motivation to work at your best. With the new acquisition, everyone is going to have to be at their best, and that means that the working environment has to be positive and inspiring.
>
> 7. Let's be very clear about what we expect from our people. We have a very dynamic and ever-changing business. Our customers are more demanding than ever before. So we really have to be extremely clear about what we expect our people to do in order to meet these challenges.
>
> 8. Let's you and I be clear on what our expectations are of each other and how we want things to be done. So, what do you expect from me? And here's what I expect from you.
>
> 9. And if I may be personal for a minute, creating that positive environment will be very valuable to you in the new organization. You're an ambitious individual, you work very hard, you have the company in your veins, you've achieved a lot and contributed much for the betterment of our organization. But the reality is that a negative working environment does everyone harm—it never leads to promotion for anyone.

The bully was surprised by her approach and definitely was taken out of his "bully boots." The how-to worked to turn this bully around. And Liz was effusive, not only because she managed the confrontation so well, but also because she was able to help a colleague change his negative and damaging behavior. The discussion was tough but positive and done in the helping mode. A difficult situation turned into a win-win for everybody. Give a hug, get a hug.

From the Shutdown Zone to the Power of Positivity

Okay, we now get that bullies should not be tolerated, but the question remains, how do you deal with tough or negative issues effectively? What do you suggest we do, GK, when somebody screws up, just makes a mess of things, and fuels the fire of anger; when bullying rears its ugly head, with the desire to lash out at the person who screwed up?

Excellent question. I'm not naïve. When mistakes are made, when problems arise, when the proverbial fan starts turning, human nature is such that people lash out, they get angry and say and do things they usually regret later. That's the conditioning that a lot of people went through. And sadly it's the only way they learned how to deal with problems. That conditioning is difficult, if not impossible, to change. However, people can learn and re-condition themselves to react differently when there are problems and mistakes. As I mentioned in an earlier chapter, behavior can be modified.

The fact is there are better ways than bullying to manage mistakes, problems and challenging issues—ways that are far more productive and certainly not as damaging to people. Flying off the handle really creates more damage than is called for—and frankly, it puts the offender in a very precarious position, despite the seeming sense of power they may feel. I've seen so many careers ruined because of it: "He's a hot head, can't handle his temper; he's always yelling at people." So here are some special guidelines to remember. They will help everyone better manage their reactions.

If you can't lift me up—please don't put me down!

If you can't praise me—please don't degrade me

If you can't accept me—please don't reject me

If you can't be kind—please don't be cruel

If you can't love me—please don't hate me

If you can't be honest—please don't lie

If you can't be a friend—please don't be a hypocrite

If you can't…—please don't…

The technique that is the most effective and most helpful to everyone involved is:

Attack the Problem, Not the Person

We've talked about that earlier, but it's worth repeating that the reason this is such an effective technique is because of what happens to a human being when they are attacked, demeaned, bullied, berated, or put down. They immediately fall into what I call, the "Shutdown Zone."

- People shut down.
- They enter a state of fear and rejection.
- Anger builds up.
- Stress and frustration increase.
- Thoughts of revenge creep into the mind.
- They retreat.
- They lose all motivation.
- Their self-esteem plummets.
- Their confidence is virtually destroyed.
- They suffer almost total paralysis.

There is nothing positive in the Shutdown Zone. It's a dark and lonely place. It's an extremely debilitating state, both for the individual and for the company. The result of this paralysis and shutdown is very costly. While many consider all this stuff to be warm and fuzzy, and others call it "the soft stuff," the fact is that there are tremendous costs exacted when people are put into the Shutdown Zone. The numbers, shown earlier, clearly demonstrate that it has a devastating impact on the bottom line. Intimidation, bullying, and all that stuff cannot, and should not, be in the lexicon of people management.

The Shutdown Zone Impact

What happened to the quality of our products?

What happened to the great service that we built our reputation on?

Why are customers complaining?

Why are the employees signing union cards?

> Where are all the creative ideas we used to get from our people?
>
> Why is it that our people are not engaged in the business?
>
> Why is it that they just seem to be going through the motions?
>
> What happened to the sense of urgency that used to drive our people to exceed expectations?
>
> Why is it that our people seem to have lost their pride in the company?
>
> Why don't they trust the leadership team?
>
> What ever happened to accountability and responsibility?
>
> Where is all that "good stuff"?

What needs to be understood and appreciated is that in the Shutdown Zone, people cannot and never will contribute their best. Period. As a manager, use the power you have to do good.

> ***Understand the Power You Have***
>
> You have the power to make people feel great.
>
> You have the power to positively impact both the head and the heart.
>
> You have the power to influence, to inspire, to motivate others to reach their full potential.
>
> You have the power to build the confidence of other people.
>
> You have the power to help others go from good to great.
>
> You have the power to raise children in a positive environment and thus ensure they have the confidence needed to take advantage of the many opportunities they will have later on in their life.
>
> You have the power to make an impact on a human being for life.
>
> You, as one single, solitary individual, have that power.

You have tremendous power to impact others in a very positive manner. Imagine, you can build their confidence, solidify their self-esteem, increase the skills they have, enhance their career, help bring out their full potential, enable the release of their creativity, inspire their initiative, and motivate them to reach new, and much higher levels of satisfaction.

All that good stuff is in your hands to do—and, frankly, I can't think of a better place to put it. As your coach, I really want the very best for you. Please remember the tremendous power you have—and use it wisely.

10
THE HUMAN FILES

In my desire to keep things simple, easy to understand, and easy to apply when it comes to understanding human behavior and how to manage people, I talk about the human mind being akin to a computer's hard drive. That hard drive contains thousands of folders, each one loaded with files from childhood to present day. If we knew what was in those files, we'd have an easy time managing and dealing with others. But we don't know, and therein lies the challenge of human behavior and of trying to understand why people say and do what they say and do.

This concept of human files will help you become better attuned to how your employees are feeling and what issues are affecting their behavior. That will help you better communicate with them so that you are helping them, not hurting them.

While we don't know what's in each person's files, we can be sure that there are good files and not-so-good ones. It's helpful to remember that fact because each day will see the opening of a variety of these files:

- A pleasant piece of music may open a feel-good file.
- A phone call about a relative's illness would open a sad file.
- Signing divorce papers will open a variety of hurt files.

What's important to note is that the individual has no choice but to react in some way to the opening of these files and, as a result, you may witness changes in their mood and in their behavior from one hour to the next. Another equally important fact is that each day will also see the creation of a variety of files, caused by interactions with others and by the activities they engage in. So in your dealings with others, please note that old files are being opened and new files are being created—each and every day.

PAST Files—Opened Daily
FUTURE Files—Created Daily

The "files" concept should be the guidepost for our interactions with others—in business, at home, even on the golf course. It makes relating to others so much easier, even better. And the benefits of using the "files" concept are numerous:

- Helps enormously in understanding human behavior.
- Provides valuable insight on why people react the way they do.
- Explains the mood they are in.
- Helps understand how they are feeling.
- Adds a new dimension to the usual question, "How are you today?"
- Explains why we should listen more attentively to what people say.
- Serves as a reminder that people's moods are shaped by every encounter and interaction. For example, the way someone is feeling at work today may be affected by files that may well have been opened on their way to the office.
- Reminds us that there will always be a blend of some good files and some not-so-good files.
- Clearly indicates the immense power that each individual has over others.
- Shows why you need to use your "file creation power" very judiciously.
- Alerts us that what we say and what we do creates "files" in the human "hard drive."

Negative in—Negative out
Positive in—Positive out

We all need to be sensitive to how our behavior is affecting those around us because both positive and negative files will stay on the individual's hard drive for life—yes, for life! Ask any golfer who has ever had a hole-in-one and they will remember every little detail of that "file," years, even decades later. They'll remember what the weather was like, exactly what club they used, who they were playing with, what they did once they realized they had a hole-in-one, and every other detail of the event. The "file" was created and it's still on the "hard drive" of that person's mind.

It's the same in the workplace. Files are created daily. A good manager makes every attempt to create positive files for the people he comes in contact with and certainly the people who report to him. The metaphorical "hug" of appreciation that we've talked about will create a positive and long-lasting file. Obviously, rejection will create a negative file. Here's an actual example from a situation I was involved in.

Ms. CH vividly remembers how her boss berated her during her annual performance review, blaming her for something she was not responsible for and not involved in. And even though she tried to convince him that he had the wrong person, Mr. T would not let up—he kept on with his attack. She burst into tears as a result and had to leave his office to compose herself. Then she had the presence of mind to get some documents to prove her point. She went back into his office and showed him the papers. I asked her what happened then. Her reply, "He sat there in utter silence and did not have the courtesy or the decency to apologize to me. And, even more disgusting, he maintained his 2 rating on me (out of 5). I had to go to human resources to fight my case. I won, they revised my rating to a 4. But I still hurt when I think of how he treated me."

She wanted my advice on what to do because she realized that working for him was impossible. No matter what she did, it seemed that he was out to get her. I told her to get out of there and find a new company, or at least a new boss to work for within the same organization. She loves her new job, working in the same company for another boss, and has already been promoted to a manager role. But the hurt file is still on her hard drive. I called her a few weeks ago and thought I'd be cute by asking her how Mr. T was doing. She laughed as she told me he had been fired. I must confess, I laughed with her. She is well on her way to an outstanding career because, fortunately, she has more positive files than negative ones on her hard drive.

On the positive side, Mr. M still remembers how his boss rushed to see him in the hospital after he had suffered a mild heart attack. The funny part of the story was that his boss was by his side even before his wife was. He laughs at that and he certainly remembers it, years later. He was obviously touched by the immediate response of his boss, "He really cared about me and wanted to help me as much as possible—whatever you need, take as much time as required for a full recovery. His attention, his kindness was truly amazing to me. It was all positive stuff I will remember for a long time."

A negative file created by a bad boss; a positive file created by a caring boss. That's the power that you, as a manager, as a parent, as a friend, have.

The Hurt Files

Here's an exercise to prove that certain negative files are imprinted in the mind for a lifetime and why I call them "hurt files."

Close your eyes and get into your own thinking mode. I guess you don't have to close your eyes if you don't want to, but I want you to think of something that happened way back when, that really hurt you. Got it? It usually takes a second or two for people to think of something.

Now let me ask you, how long ago was the event that hurt you? Ten years ago? Twenty-five years ago? Forty years ago? Or maybe it was 50 years ago? Are you in pain? Are you feeling angry? Ticked off? Getting depressed? The event *still* hurts you, doesn't it? That's why I have termed these types of files "hurt files." They hurt, and they hurt like hell.

Sorry, but I just had to do that exercise to prove how debilitating and painful these hurt files are. I've done this exercise for 35 years now with various groups. People have broken down, tears have flowed, and people have had to leave the meeting room to regain their composure. But at the end of the exercise, the most gratifying thing is that people learn and finally realize just how painful these hurt files are. Moreover, in that moment, they realize and understand that each person has the ability to create a hurt file for another individual. The more significant lesson is that each individual has the power to create a positive file, not one that hurts.

Hurt files are created by the act of doing or saying something that attacks, abuses, demeans, berates, degrades, puts down, scolds, bullies, intimidates, or threatens another human being. Even if you don't know a word about psychology, please understand this concept of hurt files and understand how serious it is. The hurt files are indelibly inscribed in the mind of the individual for life. They cannot be erased. People can go to therapy for years, but the hurt files will still be there and they will still hurt. And to reinforce this point, please allow me to share one of the many hurt files I still have on my hard drive.

I experienced this pain 58 years ago. My mother died when I was three years old, of breast cancer. We had to live with my father's mother, who in the kindest word I can find is best described as a "witch." And I say that because she beat me every day, repeat, every day. No matter what I did or what I said, she didn't like it and came after me with that black strap she always carried with her, or her favorite stick, or whatever else she could pick up quickly and use to hurt me. Anyway, here's the incident, or I should say the hurt file that is still on my hard drive.

My brother and I were sitting at the small table we had in the kitchen having lunch. As it came to pass, we both reached out for the bottle of Heinz ketchup at the same time and, as normal eight- and nine-year-olds, we began to fight over it, pulling and tugging at it back and forth. The witch saw that. She grabbed my right hand and slammed it flat on the table. Then she took a fork and began to jab the fork into my hand. Blood gushed out like a fountain. I was screaming. I fought to get away from her.

I ran out of the third-floor apartment, down the stairs screaming, yelling, crying and bleeding all over the place. I was running to my other grandmother's house a few blocks away. There was only one problem. The French gang controlled 11th Avenue and I didn't have time to go around them, as I usually did. Blood was flowing from my hand. The pain was getting worse. My screams were getting louder. I had to go through the gang's territory. They couldn't hurt me anymore than I was already hurt.

They saw me running up the street and came out of nowhere on either side. I knew I'd be in very deep trouble with them, but I just kept running through the corridor they had formed. I was doomed. I still have nightmares about that today.

Amazingly, and to this day, I haven't figured out why the gang let me through untouched. I guess they saw the blood all over me, heard my screaming and crying and concluded I had had enough hurt.

Although you can't see them, there are tears in my eyes as I write this. It was one of the most horrible experiences of my life. Even more evil than the time she picked me up by my feet and drilled my head into the stones on the ground.

Fifty-eight years later, those hurt files are as vivid as the actual time they were created. They still hurt. Fortunately, I've learned to make sure I don't click my "mouse" on those files but just quickly scroll past them.

Hurt files don't even have to be that dramatic to do lasting harm. Even a small, innocuous comment from a manager can create a hurt file for the employee. Virtually every client I've had over the years has a hurt file of some kind. The important thing is to recognize these hurt files for what they are, and develop strategies for dealing with them.

It's equally important to realize that you have the power to create positive files by helping others, by being kind to others, rather than hurting others by what you say and what you do. Think about it. Which type of file do you want to be remembered for—a hurt file or a positive file?

How to Manage the Hurt Files

As I said, we all carry hurt files around on our hard drive. What's in those files can range from little hurts to deep pain. If we spend our lives reading and rereading them, figuratively, reliving that pain over and over again, those files will debilitate us. We'll be paralyzed to move forward, to accomplish anything, and we'll never be able to be happy. So while we all have hurt files, we must learn to develop strategies for living with them, dealing with them, and managing them—actually turning them to our advantage instead of letting them destroy our lives. Following are some ways in which you can manage your own hurt files, or help employees who report to you deal with theirs.

First of all, learn to avoid opening those files. Keep the "mouse" away from them; you may see them in the "folder" but just scroll past them. Accept the hurt files for what they are. You can't erase them, so just acknowledge that they are there. Your parents, your teacher, your boss—or whoever it may have been—did what they did to you and there is nothing you can do now to right the wrong they inflicted upon you. Remember that you did nothing to deserve their treatment; you were simply a victim of their insanity and their inhumanity. You can spend the next 60 years of your life trying to rationalize what they did but it will not erase the hurt files. I'm sorry, but that's the reality. Acceptance of this fact will help you move on.

There's an old saying that what doesn't kill you makes you stronger. Despite the pain you've gone through, you are a survivor and even the worst experiences you've suffered have helped to build your character and define the strength of your character. Now use that strength to put your hurt files in their proper place—behind you. To move beyond the hurt, and be able to put it behind you, you'll need to do some work. You absolutely need to take an inventory and do an analysis of all the positive things you've accomplished over the years. Make an actual list so that you can see the good things that you've done. Go as far back as you can, right up to the present day.

Write all your accomplishments down as you think about them, in no particular order. Making this list will help you to realize just how good you really are, how talented you really are, and how excellent your track record of success has been. In addition to your accomplishments, also make a list of the qualities and competencies you demonstrated along the way. For example, you may realize that your biggest achievements are thanks in large part to your courage, tenacity, perseverance, sacrifice, diligence, discipline, sense of caring and helpfulness to others, and so on. Using the following template may help you with this exercise:

ACCOMPLISHMENTS—WHAT I DID	HOW I DID IT	MY LEARNINGS
Built high-performance team at xx, despite the fact that they were a dysfunctional group	Listening skills, negotiation skills, the human touch, integrity, was genuine throughout the process	I'm very skilled at bringing people together. I'm "real" with people.
Ignited team spirit Created culture of success Recognition, recognition, recognition	Courage, tenacity, perseverance, sacrifice, discipline, diligence, strength, caring, compassion, tears, and a lot of "counting to 10, sometimes 20"	I enjoy the creative process and all that goes with it. I like being the leader of a great team.

This analysis will reveal to you that you have developed an impressive list of attributes, skills, talents, and a record of achievement.

Now make a similar list of some of the major challenges you have faced in your life and how you dealt with them. This exercise will help you realize that you withstood and overcame all kinds of challenges along the way. You have that ability. You're not afraid of challenges. You've surpassed many of them, if not every one of them.

Okay, so we have this amazing list of positives that you have accomplished. Will that solve everything? No. But it's a major step forward, primarily because it will help you realize just how good you really are and how much you've accomplished. That's a vital technique in managing the hurt files. I want you to be very proud of *you*.

I want *you* to learn how to give yourself credit for all those good things. And I say that because you'll never be recognized for your accomplishments by the people who caused your hurt files in the first place—never.

That's a tough reality check, but you have to accept it, as tough as it is. They are not going to turn around now and become nice people or undo the hurt that they caused. Sorry to be so blunt, but it just won't happen. Your desire to be appreciated by the people who hurt you will never be realized. So, your "appreciation folder," so to speak, will always be empty when it comes to those family members, teachers, bosses—whoever they may be. You will have to look elsewhere for the appreciation you crave.

Okay, so how do you fill your appreciation folder, and make sure it stays filled? The exercise you did above clearly indicates that your expertise, your personality, and your abilities will enable you to write your own "appreciation files." First, close the book on the people who created your hurt files and start focusing on other sources—your customers, your colleagues, your friends, and others in your network. Seek out the people who give you positive feedback and good feelings—and start learning to be appreciated.

Next, make the first move with other people. Give a hug, get a hug. It's very easy to do this. All you have to do is to say and do things for these people that will engender their appreciation—and they, in turn, will fill you up. For example, as soon as you finish reading this section, write a thank-you card or letter (not an email) to someone you know. Give it to them—and listen to what their response is. Now, how do you feel? Didn't they "fill you up?" It's an easy process, isn't it?

First fill others up, and then be filled up by them. Pretty soon, your appreciation files will be overflowing. Guaranteed. The trick is that you have to initiate the action. You have to make the first move.

Tried and True Formula
Give Appreciation—Get Appreciation
Give Recognition—Get Recognition
Give a Hug—Get a Hug
Give Love—Get Love

So the message is straightforward. All interactions with other people create files on our emotional hard drive. Those files can be positive or negative. And the good news is that you can learn to manage the most negative ones, the hurt files. You can, in fact, override the negative files by loading up your hard drive with an overwhelming number of files that contain only positive content.

In that way, you have the unique opportunity to expend your time and energy doing positive things rather than trying to repair the past and living in the past. You cannot change the way you were treated growing up—but:

- You can write a thank-you card to someone right now and feel nourished by their response to your action.
- You can pick up the phone right now and call a friend and share some positive laughs together.
- You can invite one of your employees to lunch tomorrow and let them blush with appreciation for your kind gesture.
- You can take the initiative and prepare a status report highlighting all the accomplishments of your team—mention them by name and then send it to your immediate supervisor. Giving them credit for the positive things they've done demonstrates real leadership and that is a positive file—big time.

- You can get in touch with a colleague and apologize for the spat you had last week. That will surprise him and generate good files for both of you, and help both of you be more productive for the good of the business and the good of your teams. That's a lot of good files you'll create in one simple gesture.

So please stop draining your energy on the past—go create positive files now.

The Hurt Files at Work

In many ways, the hurt file zone is the major consequence of poor management of people and relationships. It's the final outcome, the dangerous consequence, if you wish, of what happens when people are put down, regardless of the manner in which that's done.

As mentioned earlier, when people are attacked, or when hurt files are created, they have no choice but to go into the hurt file prison. There is nothing positive there. It's a dark and lonely place. It's an extremely debilitating state for the individual and it's damaging for the company. From a business point of view, it is an extremely costly place for employees to be in—billions of dollars a year are wasted because people are in that prison.

For many, it's a prison they just don't know how to get out of. Many find themselves in that prison for life, and most have no idea of what it is that's holding them back or why their potential has been stolen from them. The fact is, in that hurt-files prison, they are robbed of their confidence, their self-esteem, their worth, their validity—robbed of everything.

What a shame. It's a major tragedy and a total waste of human potential. It drives people to drink, to get into drugs and all the other escapes. And how can you blame them? People have to do something to ease the pain of being in that prison.

So in my own way, I'm hoping that this book, that these words and phrases, these discussions, will help managers to avoid putting others into that hurt file prison by what they say or what they do.

Here's a real example to consider. Sandra is a manager who is a highly competent individual when it comes to the technical aspects of her profession. In fact, she has her PhD in the field. She's super bright, intelligent, loved by her external customers, well-spoken, and presents herself very well to senior management. She manages about a hundred people and has done so for almost fifteen years.

Her boss, the VP of the Division, told me, and I quote, "She is a uniquely qualified individual who would be very hard to replace. We're lucky to have such an expert in our company."

I replied, "That sounds wonderful. It seems like you have an ideal manager? Why have you called me? How can I help you?"

> "She's excellent in the technical aspects of the job, in my opinion. Except that recently, someone she manages finally blew the whistle on her treatment of the people in the department and launched a formal complaint of 'psychological abuse and bullying' with the human resource department. We want you to talk to the person who complained and find out what is going on. Give us your professional opinion on what we should do."

So, we arranged for me to meet with the complainant in order to get a pulse on how severe the problem was. The fact is, it's easier to talk to an outsider in a confidential manner than to talk to a company representative. We're able to get into the issues at a much deeper level and thus discover far more helpful information, upon which we can make more accurate assessments and provide more actionable direction to the company. And we listen without being judgmental or becoming emotional. The discussion was, in a word, unbelievable. Here's some of what I was told.

> "She treats us like kids. She yells at us, she scolds us, she berates us constantly. No matter what we do, she seems to always find fault with it; she's always correcting us. She uses language that is not becoming of a professional in our field. She even makes people cry. We have such high turnover because of the bullying tactics she uses. We're all professionally trained and educated people, yet she is constantly putting us down.
>
> "We've had it with her; something has to be done about her. The more senior people in the department are afraid to speak up; they

don't want to lose their jobs and they know that she will let them have it. I'm the newest kid on the block so I decided to speak up for the others. I'm not afraid of her. The company has to do something about her."

I decided to interview several other people to confirm what I had heard and verify just how bad it really was. It was indeed a very bad situation. This kind of behavior had been going on for years and no one had the courage to say or do anything about it.

The result is that the people in the department were in the hurt file prison. It is critical to understand that this emotional prison is full of fear. It's void of any courage. Whatever strength an individual may have had is sapped out of them. They shut up, fearing they'll lose their job and fearing further recrimination and reprisal.

The work in the department had dwindled. All kinds of mistakes were being made. Morale was bad. And a formal complaint for abuse and bullying was lodged.

Obviously, the alarm bells went off and the president, the VP of HR and the VP of the division met with me to go over my report. After a three-hour session, the decision was made to take Sandra out of the department and give her a different job within the company, without people management responsibilities. In order to make it palatable to her they gave her a fancy "director" title.

What's amazing about this true story is that Sandra's behavior and poor style of people management was tolerated for so long by her bosses. The justification for their not dealing with the problem was that she had specialized technical skills that were hard to replace.

Well, after 15 years, and thanks to the courageous employee who brought the matter to the attention of senior management, the employees who worked for her finally had relief. For them, it was a breath of fresh air:

- Their productivity increased.
- The quality of their work improved.
- Mistakes were dramatically reduced.
- The working environment became refreshingly positive.

However, for Sandra, this course of action won't help her a bit. Her behavior won't change because her ego and her arrogance were never addressed in the first few years of her employment. She felt she had the right to deal with her people the way she saw fit. In her mind, she saw nothing wrong with how she was managing people. Remember what we said earlier: condone poor behavior, get poor behavior.

The real shame of this story is that her boss was too afraid to address her behavior with her. What should have been done as soon as he found out about how she was managing her people, is to sit her down and have a meeting about how to modify her behavior. He should have levelled with her and been very clear that his expectations were that she treat people with the highest degree of respect; that poor treatment of them would not be tolerated regardless of her title; and that abusive behavior of any kind was immediate grounds for dismissal.

Instead of doing that, his own fears crept in and nothing, absolutely nothing, was done. He could have helped her become a well-rounded manager, who would have been able to combine her technical prowess with much better people management skills—a powerful combination that would have elevated her to new heights of success and satisfaction. Frankly, he shirked his responsibilities and in doing so, created a disaster for the department, for the people in the department, for the company, and for Sandra who, in a sense, was the victim of his inaction and insecurity. What a shame.

Eliminating the Hurt Files at Work

Take steps to correct poor people management immediately, as soon as you hear about it. Do not put it off; deal with it.

Manage by being in helping mode rather than confrontation mode.

If needed, create a code of conduct for your team and adhere to it.

Conduct regular meetings with your people to ensure they are being treated with respect and no hurt files are being created.

Meet quarterly with your managers to review their people and determine how they are being managed.

Insist on having a high-performance culture.

Insist on having an open communication policy where people are free to contribute ideas and suggestions, without the fear of reprisal.

Insist on having a positive working environment that is focused on making the business better.

Ensure that everyone knows that abusive behavior is grounds for dismissal.

Discuss the concept of hurt files and insist that everyone avoids creating them; have a zero tolerance for hurt files.

11

SIMPLE TRUTHS FOR MANAGING PEOPLE

At this point you should have a good understanding of how much harm rejection, bullying, intimidation, and downright bad people management can do to individual employees and to the organization as a whole. And you should also have a good idea of how effective recognition and appreciation can be as a management practice, as well as how to implement them into your daily management routine. In this chapter, we'll delve a little further into how you can better understand human behavior and practice recognizing people in order to help them realize their full potential.

I'm constantly asked if there is an easy way to understand people. My usual answer is that there is an easier way than most people realize. Managing people can be very complex. No doubt about that. And it's made even more so because in the business world, generally, there is a deficiency of knowledge about what makes people tick, about what the human motivating factors are, and a lack of understanding about human behavior in general.

The fact is most people have not taken a psychology or human behavior course. In fact, most people run away as fast as they can from the word "psychology." The other startling fact is that these courses are not usually part of any curriculum in the business schools.

Managers learn how to manage people on the job. They copy the way they were managed by previous bosses or they just go on instinct, using their own upbringing as their guide on what to do and what not to do. And we've seen how horribly wrong that can go.

The other reality in business is that most managers turn their people issues over to the human resources department. Thus they don't have to get into the subject of people at all, rationalizing, "That's HR's responsibility, not mine." So, is there anything wrong with any of that? Not really, I suppose, "It is what it is."

"It is what it is" is a reality. But I believe that each reality comes with an opportunity—an opportunity to improve things, to make things better, to seek new learning, to try new things, to make the job of managing much easier, and to derive a much greater sense of satisfaction from one's work and one's life.

So how do you make all this happen? There are numerous ways of doing this, of course, but in this chapter I'd like to focus on some of the simplest, quickest, and most effective ways I want to call these "simple truths," primarily because they are very simple to apply immediately, and they have proven to generate great results.

Simple Truth One: We Share a Lot of Common Needs and Desires

The first simple truth is truly foundational. For all our individual differences, we are fundamentally all the same, sharing common needs and desires. That means that the people you manage have more or less the very same desires you have. Furthermore, what motivates us is common to all people. Consider the following;

- We all want to be loved.
- We all want to be appreciated for what we do.
- We all enjoy positive attention.
- We all want more money.
- We all want to achieve.
- We all want to feel like we've done something worthwhile.
- We all want our children to grow up and have a good life.
- We all want to have nice things.
- We all want to derive a sense of satisfaction from our lives.
- We all want to be happy, however that is defined.
- And for us golfers, we all fantasize about getting a hole-in-one.

When you look at it that way, understanding what makes people tick and understanding how to manage people is not as difficult or as complex as it has been made out to be.

The unassailable fact is that at our core, we are more alike than we are different. It's easy to forget that, especially when we manage others. Remember that your employees have the same needs as you do. Do you enjoy being put down—then why put others down? Do you feel good when your boss tells you you've done a great job—then tell your employees they've done a great job. And so on. It's really quite simple to understand and to apply this truth, isn't it?

Yet somehow, it's taken for granted. Perhaps it's because many people are busy trying to make themselves feel somehow above, bigger, or better than the other person. That quest has greatly diminished the importance of paying attention to people and the manner in which they are managed.

Managers get annoyed by individual idiosyncrasies, criticize when someone doesn't approach a problem the way they would, or berate an employee for making a mistake because they don't have the same knowledge or experience. But the fact is—and this should be at the very foundation of every manager's understanding—we are more alike than not; we share common objectives; and we can achieve so much more by working together and managing others in a supportive and collaborative manner. To put it in other words, it's People Management 101—it's fundamental. Here are some phrases I want you to remember:

Our human needs are the same—our experiences are different

Our human needs are the same—our upbringing is different

Our human needs are the same—our education is different

Our human needs are the same—our trappings are different

Our human needs are the same—our styles are different

Our human needs are the same—our methods are different

Our human needs are the same—our ideologies are different

Our human needs are the same—our beliefs are different

Our human needs are the same—our skill sets are different

The very important point is that in the management of people it is essential to pay attention to the human needs that make us alike, and to respect those elements that distinguish us from each other.

Here's the problem many managers get into. They assume that everyone around them should have the same skills and experiences that they have, and even more shocking, many actually believe that their way is the right way, some even think it's the only way.

To be an effective manager, it is vital to respect the differences between people, and to understand that despite those differences, they are still motivated and inspired and encouraged by the fundamental human needs that we all have in common. Remembering that we are basically all the same will help to remind us that we should treat others the way we ourselves would like to be treated. That's key to being, or becoming, a great people manager.

Simple Truth Two: Be a Good Listener

The importance of listening, as a manager, as a parent, as just a person having a normal conversation, is absolutely vital. Yet despite that seemingly obvious fact, most people don't pay enough attention to listening—and most don't know how to listen.

Why is it that way? It's simply the fact that we are conditioned to react to what we hear, rather than taking an extra second or so to think about what has just been said. It's essential to first understand what is meant by what is being said, before we respond. The fact is that most people are not masters of communication. They use words and phrases that often hide or disguise what they truly mean and what they truly want from you.

Here's a tried-and-true principle to keep in mind when learning how to become a better listener.

The Iceberg Principle

What people actually say is not necessarily what they really mean.

> *What a person says is like an iceberg: you see only 20 percent of it on the surface(what they say). The rest of the iceberg, 80 percent of it, is below the surface of the water (what they really mean).*

Therefore, the real art of listening is being able to clarify and understand what the person really means and then, and only then, respond to that meaning, rather than responding to the exact words being spoken. Yes, that will take a minute or so more than you're used to, but rest assured, it will make you a much better listener. For example:

What is Said = *"I'd like to bounce an idea off you."*
What is Meant = *"I'd like your approval and encouragement on this idea because I don't want to develop something that will not be accepted and will, therefore, make me feel like a failure."*

OR it could mean = *"The last time I submitted an idea I was shot down and made to look stupid, so I don't want to be in that position again."*

OR it could mean = *"People around here are critical, sometimes mean. I don't like to be shot down in public, so I need your support before I mention this idea at our next meeting."*

Obviously, the response to each of these meanings should be different. Responding appropriately shows you've really listened to the individual and tailored your response to their needs.

A Good Listening Process

1. The person asks a question, or simply says something.
2. Respond by saying something like, "That's interesting," or, "That's a good question," "Thanks for asking that." All the while you're thinking, "I wonder what they mean by that?" What this does is to acknowledge and respect the person who has asked the question. It's a positive reaction.

3. Now start asking questions to obtain clarification before you answer. Use the "1,001 questions" technique. Asking questions and letting the other person speak is an incredibly powerful way to be a better listener.

   By the way, "how" questions are the best in order to get the other person to clarify what they mean. How questions are open-ended, which will get the other person talking and explaining more fully, rather than simply giving one-word answers.

   > - How would you make that happen?
   > - How would you like me to help?
   > - How would you suggest we manage that situation?
   > - How do you think they'll respond to that approach?
   > - How would you address that?
   > - How will the presentation make things better?
   > - How will the other departments react to this?

4. Ask as many questions as you have to in order to fully understand where the other individual is coming from, what he means, what he may be after, his motive for asking, and so on. This shows that you are engaged. You care about providing a well-thought-out response, rather than simply a knee-jerk reaction. You are giving the person the recognition and the attention they hope for. You're validating them and validating the importance of their question.
5. Respond: By now you may have figured out what they mean, so respond to that, and thank them for asking the question, or making the statement.

It may not be immediately obvious to you, but the art of listening is very closely related to the topic of giving recognition, because you are validating the person; you're thanking them for asking the question or making the statement; you're demonstrating respect for their thoughts, their ideas, their point of view, and so on, all of which we have spent so much time emphasizing.

People need to share their thoughts, especially with a person of a higher rank, because they want that person's approval, reinforcement, and encouragement—all of which are dimensions of recognition. Being a good listener is a strong demonstration that you are paying attention to your people; that you care about the person; that you respect what they have to say; that you care enough to get them engaged and are prepared to listen to what they have to say, and in so doing, you're giving them that "hug" that will motivate and inspire them.

Simple Truth Three: Appeal to the Head and the Heart

The next helpful realization is the seemingly obvious truth that every individual is composed of two key elements that guide their every action:

The head, the rational part
The heart, the emotional component

That truth may be obvious, but it is most often overlooked when it comes to managing and dealing with people.

In business, the rational needs are straightforward: the numbers, the goals, the cases sold, the displays, the merchandising, product knowledge, presentation skills, writing skills, EPS, category management, computer skills, negotiation skills, and so on. These talents are the basic requirements of the job that the employee has to possess. They become the measurements of the individual's success.

The emotional elements are less evident than the rational ones and usually receive less attention in the business world. Part of the reason is that the emotional side is perceived by many as a soft topic and the business world generally doesn't like anything soft or mushy.

> *"We only deal with the facts, the numbers, the top line, the bottom line, so stay away from that mushy stuff, we're not here to hug and kiss people."*

Yet these same people want *respect* from their people; they talk about corporate *values*, about how *impressed* they are with so and so, about the importance of *honesty* and *trust* and *integrity*, and the fact that people are the *lifeblood* of the organization. Not a single executive would deny the importance of these attributes. Yet all the words in italics are emotional words. *They have to do with the heart, not the head.* Please remember, the head thinks about what to do—the heart drives us to do it.

The truth is that if enough attention is paid to both head and heart elements, if they are both stimulated, attended to, and given their proper due, then the management of people in business and in daily life would be that much easier and far more rewarding. Is it that simple? I truly believe it is—really!

A relatively easy way to address the heart side of the business equation is to make an emotional connection with the people you interact with, and do that as follows:

- Build their confidence
- Provide encouragement
- Be supportive
- Be inspiring
- Engender a sense of pride
- Promote a positive team spirit
- Be engaged in what they do and how they do it
- Demonstrate understanding and caring when personal issues arise
- Foster open communication—allow them expression
- Seek their input and feedback which validates their views
- Listen attentively—respond and be thankful for what they say
- Expand your personal knowledge of them
- Treat people with respect
- Recognize personal and family milestones
- Never bully, intimidate, berate
- Show appreciation for effort as well as results
- Consistently recognize success

All of which means, of course, "Give 'em a hug!" In fact, this concept of appealing to the heart with an emotional connection is very useful in other situations:

- Sales people are well advised to establish an emotional connection with their customers.

- Internal departments will get along together much better if an emotional connection between them has been established.
- Real teamwork can only exist if there is a strong emotional connection between the members of the team.

To reinforce a point made earlier, there is nothing mushy or soft about this emotional connection thing. In fact, the stronger the connection, the stronger the motivation to achieve exceptional results and exceptional productivity.

Let's be clear. There's no doubt that the head stuff is crucial to the success of any business, any endeavour. But focusing on just the head stuff absolutely limits the realization of the full human potential available. Bringing out the best in people and getting them to perform at their peak potential requires that we pay attention, even nurture, both the head and the heart. The person who does both is usually a great leader and reaps the resultant rewards.

In order to realize an individual's full potential, you have to manage both elements, the head and the heart. If you focus on the rational side only, the head, you'll probably get good stuff, but you'll never get the great stuff. And in today's world, good is not good enough. Moreover, why would you just settle for good when great is so easily attainable?

The best example I can give of tapping into that potential is what we see time and again in the world of sports. Teams that were never given a chance to make it to the playoffs suddenly kick into gear, take their play to a higher level, and win everything. They are usually called Cinderella teams; I prefer to call them teams with heart. They win because they play with passion, with a positive attitude, with pride, and with that inner drive that energizes them and brings out their very best. The heart stuff drives them to win.

What about the head stuff you ask, the technical skills of the game, the plan, the charts, and the numbers? Obviously the players have to know how to play the game, but that is not the reason they win it all. The real reason is the heart they put into the game, that emotional quotient that drives them from game to game. It's the heart stuff that enlivens them, that gives them a new sense of power and a real feeling that they can overcome any obstacles. They seem to play with renewed determination, with courage, with pride, and with that famous "we can do it" attitude. All that is heart stuff. It's hard to measure, hard to put on a graph or a slide, hard to quantify, but speak to any coach and they'll all say the same thing, "They won because they played with heart."

The point of this discussion is to encourage you to seriously consider and implement your own comfortable balance between appealing to the head and the heart of each of your employees. I use the word "comfortable" because the fact is that not every manager is conditioned to manage both.

That's okay, but please understand that the balance between head and heart will vary from individual to individual, and from situation to situation. But if you want great performance, you've got to say and do something for both head and heart. It's not enough to do one or the other; you've got to do both. That will make you a better manager and a great leader. A few examples:

"I just wanted to tell you that I appreciate the personal sacrifice you made by coming in on the weekend to work on the UNICEF campaign."

"I know your daughter's graduation is on Friday. I think you should be with her. We'll cover for you if something comes up."

The other way to understand this heart stuff is to consider some of these questions:

- Are you interested in the individual's life in general?
- Are you aware of the composition of their family?
- Is he or she involved in community and charitable works?
- What are some of their hobbies and how involved are they in them?
- What are they passionate about outside of work?
- What is their major source of self-esteem?
- What are they most proud of?
- What are their most pressing challenges?
- What are their ambitions?

Understanding the heart side of the individual will provide you with numerous opportunities to give your people the metaphorical "hug" they need, and thus make you a better manager and a better leader.

Most Already Do the Heart Stuff—But Forget to Do It at Work

Interestingly, people pay attention to the matters of the heart in their personal lives with friends, family, children, spouse, lover, and so on. But what is amazing to me is that as soon as they walk into their workplace, they tend to forget the heart stuff. It's as if they never heard of it, didn't know it was there. I hear things like, "I'm not paid to get involved with that. Don't bother me with that warm and fuzzy crap."

Regardless of what those feelings may be, I want to encourage everyone to consider the powerful impact you can make on another person by addressing some of the heart matters. With a little effort and the use of some simple techniques, you can, and will, better manage people, better manage business, and better manage yourself.

What I want you to do is to look in a mirror and realize that you, yourself, are made up of both sides, head and heart. Now think about how much impact both elements have on your drive, your motivation, your moods, your moments of joy, the times that you were totally ticked off and the times you were totally fired up.

Look in the mirror and ask yourself, why is it that some days you're on top of the world, yet on other days, you feel like you're in "cockroach city," crawling around looking for a crumb that resembles a positive something? Chances are that the answer has to do with the heart stuff. Wanting to be appreciated for all the work you do; wanting to be acknowledged for the kindness you've shown family members; wanting to belong, wanting to be cool—are all matters of the heart. There are no charts, or numbers, or PowerPoint slides for any of this.

Well guess what. The people you work with and manage seek the same validation and acceptance as you do. I suggest to all my clients that they buy a mirror and put it on their desk so they see it every day as a reminder that the people they work with are motivated and inspired by the same heart stuff they want. Everyone you interact with feels the same way you do and will have the same motivations as you do. Your wanting to be accepted is the same as their need to be accepted by you. You want to please your boss; they want to please you. That's what the mirror should remind you of each and every day.

Remember the expression, "It's the economy, stupid?" Well if you'll indulge me a little room here, let me say with all due respect, "It's the heart stuff..." that will help make you a better manager and lead your team to achieve great results. This all goes back to the first principle in this chapter, that fundamentally we are all the same. Your people are motivated by the same matters of the heart that inspire and motivate you.

The distinction between head and heart is simple to understand but, admittedly, paying attention to both seems to be much more difficult to put into practice. While the business equation is skewed to the head stuff, a good leader knows and pays attention to the heart stuff. It will enable you and your people to realize new heights of performance and satisfaction—so enjoy the success this simple truth about head and heart will generate.

Simple Truth Four: Make the Most of the Annual Performance Review

Another simple way to generate top performance from employees is to use to best effect the forum that almost every organization has for providing formal feedback to employees, the annual performance review. It's standard procedure in virtually every company. However, in my experience with both managers and employees, I must note that the power of the annual performance review is not being maximized and not being used for its intended purpose. Indeed, rather than being a helpful and positive exercise, it has, in many organizations, become a hurtful and negative one. Why do I say that? Please consider these observations:

- Many managers treat the review more like an annual report card in which they highlight all the errors and poor performance of the individual. It's the wrong approach and frankly, the wrong psychology. Sadly, most managers have never taken a human behavior course, so how would they know any better. Yet here they are playing judge and jury with another person's life.

- It should be, and needs to be, a developmental vehicle that inspires. Seen and treated as such, it becomes a special moment in the person's life, not something they dread because they feel that they will be at a trial where they will have to listen to all kinds of negatives being hurled at them.
- The next concern is that many managers see the performance review as a dull, inconvenient, and even unpleasant task that they have to do. I'm sure I don't have to describe what kind of attitude that is. It can be made better with an enthusiastic approach, one that is focused on helping the person and giving them the motivation needed to develop their skills and become a better employee.
- The annual performance review can be made much better if the manager approaches the event as an opportunity to unlock the potential of their employees. It's a moment for growth and development that highlights the positive skills of the person and how these skills were used to make the business stronger and better, and the importance of honing these skills to ensure future growth and development.

No doubt, there are some readers who are now thinking, "What about the errors and mistakes and poor performance stuff? Aren't we supposed to highlight those areas? After all, there's a section on the form called 'Areas for Improvement'—shouldn't that be filled out?"

Here's my answer to those questions as well as a strong suggestion to help you become a better manager. (By the way, the people in the HR department won't like what I have to say.) First, mistakes, errors and incidents of poor performance should be addressed and corrected and the employee coached through them at the time they occur, not six, or eight or nine months later.

> *"It serves no purpose whatsoever to tell me in December about a mistake I made back in March. I honestly don't remember the details and there's nothing I can do about it now, except to try to cope with the rejection my boss just laid on me."*

Furthermore, each mistake that a person makes is "a coaching opportunity." A good manager never lets that opportunity slip away. So address the error right away and forget the "Areas for Improvement" section on the review form.

Addressing issues immediately enables both parties to ensure that they are aligned on the objectives and on how things are being executed. It provides a great opportunity to course-correct, if required, and gives the boss the occasion to recognize and reinforce the good work that's being done.

The fact is that more frequent feedback is forward-looking and developmental. It's helpful. It's actionable. It improves productivity. It keeps supervisor and employee aligned and focused on the key objectives of the business. It makes for a much stronger and more positive working environment. More frequent feedback helps to achieve the desired results effectively and efficiently, and thus it creates that all-important culture of success. It's a well-known fact that success breeds success. So supplement the feedback you give in the annual performance review with ongoing coaching and specific feedback throughout the year to make the most of developmental opportunities and to bring out the best in your people.

My next issue with annual reviews is what many managers have told me over the years when this topic of annual performance reviews comes up in our sessions, "It is what it is, you just fill out the form and send it to HR."

If "that's just the way it is," then I say fine. Well, maybe not so fine. I just think we can do better, especially if we truly want to create a high-performance culture and generate great results. That will come about only if we have high-performance individuals. And, as we've discussed earlier, that means we have to pay attention to both head and heart matters of employees. You just can't do one without the other and expect superior results. You'll get good results, but why not go for great results? Here are the simple truths to remember when doing performance reviews:

The "head stuff" is all about what to do.

The "heart stuff" is all about the motivation to do it.

Remember—"they won because they played with heart."

Make the annual review an uplifting and positive experience.

One more comment, please: *The real purpose of the Annual Performance Review is to give your people a great big "HUG."*

Let me reinforce another key point about these reviews. The usual focus on the negatives is not only depressing but very debilitating. The employee is not encouraged or motivated by that. And where's the appreciation for all the good work that was done during the year?

Here's another well-known fact: building on the skills and talents of the individual is a forward-looking approach, and is far more effective than the backward-looking report-card approach, which highlights the negatives of an individual. So please, if you've addressed the errors as they happened during the year, then the annual performance review should focus on the future, on those skills and talents the individual has that can add to the success of the department, that can help make things better and that will contribute to the growth and development of the company and the individual. That's forward-looking.

I don't want backward-looking feelings in the workplace. I want all hands on deck, working together to achieve the targets we've set, and enjoying the success we will have doing it. No one is perfect, no one has all the skills required, but the team usually does have all the skills needed to achieve success.

The key fact is that every human being has skills and talents that I want to combine with the other skills of the other members of the team and then use this basket of skills to move the business forward. That's why I hired each individual in the first place. I knew they didn't have it all individually, but I also knew that when combined with the other skills of the team, I had the winning formula needed to achieve greatness.

And above all, remember the immense power you have over the person and the enormous impact you have over that person's life. Use your power to help the individual realize their full potential. That's leadership. Sorry, that's great leadership!

Simple Truth Five: Clarity of Expectations

As we've already talked about, wanting to please is a fundamental human motivation—everyone wants to do that, be it to please their parents, their teachers, their friends, their families and, of course, their boss. But what is also fundamental is that in order to please, you first need to know what the expectations of you are.

It is, therefore, absolutely vital that you, as the manager, explain and clarify exactly what your expectations are—and that should include both the technical aspects, and what I call the style aspects of the work to be done. The more definitive you are, the better the results will be.

Clarity of expectations is an absolute must. Yet it is most often taken for granted, brushed aside with all kinds of assumptions and phrases such as, "It's obvious what I want," or, "They should know what is expected of them."

If you haven't told people what it is that you expect, how would they know? Why would you assume that they know what your expectations are? How would they know how to please you? I'm sure you've heard this phrase before, if not said it yourself, "No matter what I do, they're never pleased." They, whoever "they" are, are never pleased because you don't really know exactly what they want, or what their expectations are.

And the best example of clear expectations in action is in the sports world. For example, in golf, the expectation is that you get on the green in two shots, then take two putts and you will have met the "expectations" of that hole. Beat the other team by one goal, and you will have met the expectations of the hockey game, and so on. There are no assumptions and no guessing about what needs to be done. Do it and you'll win, you'll meet the expectation, and you'll get your "hug." It should be the same in the workplace.

If you don't make it clear to those who work for you what you expect from them, how can you realistically expect to recognize them effectively for a job well done?

Remember, people understand that it is only by pleasing that they will be recognized and appreciated. They need to hear that they have pleased you; that they have met, or even surpassed, your expectations. That's a confidence builder and they'll be motivated to keep pleasing you because they know you'll give them that "hug" they need. Here's a suggested flow that may help you with this clarity of expectations technique:

- Describe the issue; ensure that the big picture is clear.
- Explain what needs to be done.

- Explain why it needs to be done; ensure clarity with context.
- Then turn the matter over to the individual (or the team).
- The how-to part of resolving the issue is up to the individual.
- The individual prepares an action plan, complete with details on how they will resolve and address the issue.
- Reconvene at a prescribed time to review the plan the individual has prepared; this is an important step in making sure that your expectations are aligned.
- Adjust, modify, and finally agree to the plan.
- Acknowledge the effort made by the person and express confidence that their actions will lead to better performance.
- Set a time for follow-up, which allows for course correction, if required.
- Recognize and praise the individual for the progress being made.

Clarity of expectations is an absolute must in the management of people. It ensures that everyone on the team is fully aligned with what needs to be done to generate great results. Clear expectations help minimize mistakes and errors. And equally important, they make the recognition part of the process that much more significant and far more rewarding.

Simple Truth Six: Don't Be a Micro-Manager

Don't tell your people what you need them to do and then watch them like a hawk as they set out to do it. Why?

Micro-management greatly diminishes employee confidence

You may think that by controlling every step of the process and how it is done you are helping to ensure success, but the message you are really communicating to your people by micro-managing is that you have no faith that they can do the job you've asked them to do to your satisfaction. By your actions, you are letting them know that you disapprove of their work and how they do it. You don't even have to say a word to make them feel rejected and disengaged!

In truth, it is not the employee who is at fault in this situation. As we have seen, they are usually more than willing to help and please their manager. But micro-managers are almost impossible to please:

- They are basically insecure people.
- They are afraid of making mistakes.
- They are perfectionists who want things done their way or no way, and actually believe that their way is the best way.
- They don't trust anyone.
- They may have the title of leader, but haven't yet understood what real leadership is all about.
- They are very hard on themselves.
- They are not pleasant to work for, or to work with.

If you have a tendency to tell people exactly how you expect them to do every step of the tasks you lay out for them, then you need to nip that in the bud as quickly as possible, or you will have some very disgruntled and demoralized employees on your hands. Here are some suggestions that will help you break the habit of micro-managing:

- The clarity of expectations technique, described above, is designed to help you stop being a micro-manager and give you more time to demonstrate your leadership skills. Sorry, but you can't be a leader if you are a micro-manager. You won't have to micro-manage if you've outlined your expectations clearly. Ensure that you describe the outcomes you desire.
- Once you and your employees understand the requirements of the tasks to be done, you won't have to monitor their every move. That will give you more time to think about revenue-generating activities to grow the business, rather than being a "police officer."
- Please note that process discussions usually end up in choking the employee and robbing them of their own style—and that's not a good way to manage others. You want the objectives met and, frankly, it doesn't matter if they use red or blue, so to speak, to hit the target. Allow the employee to use their own creativity,

their own style and their own methods of achieving the desired outcome.
- By being a micro-manager, you lose the opportunity to coach your people, to boost their confidence, to improve their skills, to keep adding to their knowledge base, to give them a sense of ownership, to develop that all-important sense of responsibility and accountability, and to create a sense of urgency within your employees to execute the solution.
- There is nothing more powerful to build confidence in someone than to express simple phrases like, "I had every confidence that you'd be able to solve this. Well done," or, "You're awesome! Your solution worked very well; I'm proud of you."

So don't be a micro-manager, please. Become a great leader.

Simple Truth Seven: Develop Ownership

"Ownership" is another one of those words that pops up in most business discussions, "We want our people to have ownership in what they're doing; to think for themselves; to become solution-providers in the day-to-day challenges of business."

It sounds good. It's a great ambition. The question is, how can your people feel responsible and take ownership when you're always doing and fixing things for them, or being a micro-manager as we've just discussed?

Here's a simple technique that will enable you to help your people develop a sense of ownership in what they do; to be responsible and accountable for what they do; and to heighten the confidence they have in their own abilities.

Usually when a situation arises, the employee will run into your office and ask, "What do you want me to do?" or, "How do you want to handle this, boss?" Obviously, they don't have ownership of the matter, they want you to handle it. Or they don't have the confidence to manage it. Or they are afraid of making a mistake, or they just haven't taken the time to think about the matter and want to dump it on your lap. Whatever the reality is, we want to ensure that the employee resolves things by taking ownership of the situation and being responsible for it.

And as a manager, you also want to know if they truly have the abilities to handle the matter. Or, to put it in other words, you need to know what kind of stuff they are made of. In any case, here's how to manage the matter. All you have to say is:

> *"If you'd like to discuss a problem or, in some cases, complain about something, that's okay by me as long as you also present two possible solutions that you have thought about to resolve the issue and how you'll go about managing it."*

This two-for-one technique forces the person to think about solutions, think about how he would address the problem, and prepare himself before rushing into your office and dumping things on your desk. Let them talk. Your role is to listen to what they have to present. And even though you might have the solution, don't say a word. Stick to the principles of this two-for-one ownership technique. It's his issue. He has to solve it. Your role is to ask 1,001 questions. We talked about that earlier.

The 1,001 questions technique is a very effective method of getting people involved and engaged in a situation, in the resolution of a problem, in generating ideas, in empowering others, in fostering a sense of ownership, and in gaining their commitment to take action.

More often than not, managers just spew out the solution they want, the how-to of their choice, their way of doing things. They don't consider the other person's possible solutions or methods. In these situations, the opportunity to build the other person's confidence is lost. And ownership can never be achieved if the boss is always fixing things.

It may well be that the other person's how-to, is more effective and more productive. But we'll never know that if we don't take the time to ask "1,001 Questions," if we don't take the time to really listen to the other person. We talk about empowering others, about fostering open communications, about engaging others, yet how can that possibly happen if we don't take the time and make the effort to solicit their views, their ideas, and their thoughts? As a result, people just do what they're told to do without thinking, without considering other alternatives or possible solutions, without a search for more effective, more efficient methods. Too often the unspoken communication they get from their manager is more like, "Just do your job and shut up."

The two-for-one technique forces the individual to think about the situation and the two ways he would resolve it. Notice that I said two solutions, because that pushes the person to get into the habit of expanding their thoughts and trains them not to accept the first thing that comes to their mind. In essence, what you are doing as the manager is taking full advantage of the coaching moment that is before you.

The two-for-one technique is a proven and effective way of empowering people and, more important, of developing people to think about and take ownership of their actions. But let me be very clear, it does take a little more time and a little more effort at the outset. However, once people are used to this two-for-one principle, it actually saves time and makes things far more efficient, more productive, and far more satisfying for everyone:

- It's a major shift in attitude.
- It generates ownership.
- It's far more positive.
- It generates pride.
- It heightens achievement and satisfaction.
- It makes the person feel engaged and able to say, "I did it."

It's all sweet music for the bottom line, for your leadership, and for building the confidence level of your people.

Simple Truth Eight: The Traffic Lights
Another simple yet very effective way of better understanding human behavior and, thus, how to manage people better, is to realize that everything we all say or do falls into the "Traffic Light Zones."

Red Light: The Negative Zone
Yellow Light: The Neutral Zone
Green Light: The Positive Zone

We see traffic signals every day, so this concept can be very helpful in improving the way you communicate with and manage employees. Simply think of these traffic light zones every time you are about to say or do something that will affect another person. Keeping the image of the traffic lights in mind, you will know beforehand that what you are about to communicate will be in one of the zones. Every manager, every individual needs to ask, "What kind of zone will I put the other person into with what I am about to say or do?"

It will make things so much easier in your interactions with the people you come in contact with. Let me share some examples with you to clarify how this traffic light thing works.

Red Zone:

"I'm getting very tired of your attitude; you complain about everything around here. If you're not happy with how this company runs things, why not get out? I'm sick of your attitude."

"I need to talk to you about the presentation you gave yesterday. What in heaven's name were you thinking? Where were you coming from? What the hell was your point? You confused everyone and the jab at the salesforce was just terrible. What was that about? The sales people are doing their best and they don't deserve the hit you gave them."

"If you continue missing deadlines, we are going to have a discussion of a very different nature, and you're not going to like it. Get with the program. It's Friday at 3:00 p.m. around here, or else."

"You missed the deadline we agreed to. I don't care what's going on, you need to work on that this Saturday. I have to present that at the executive meeting on Monday afternoon."

Yellow Zone:

"That's an interesting viewpoint. I'll have to think about it and get back to you."

"You and Jennifer have to get together today or tomorrow and resolve that issue. It's important, so get to it."

"I need those slides by 3:00 p.m., so I need you to work on them right away."

Green Zone:
"The speech you gave yesterday was outstanding, very well done. I want you to think of how you could have shaved off a few minutes to make it tighter."

"A rich heritage, a solid reputation, and a track record of immense success—that's what you and your people have achieved over the years and I'm very grateful for this opportunity to share some thoughts on SAP with you. I'm delighted to be with you."

"This is an outstanding quarter; the results clearly indicate the incredible creativity and dedication that you all have. You sure make my job much easier. I sleep very well at night, knowing that I work with such a fantastic team."

The point is that whatever you say or do will fall into one of the Traffic Light Zones. The obvious recommendation is to stay in either the yellow neutral zone or the green positive zone. Why? Simply because you'll achieve so much more from your people. We've talked about the impact you have. So because of that impact, you want to avoid putting people into the red zone. It should be avoided at all costs for the reasons we've discussed.

In order to stay out of the red zone, it may help to think about the key message that you're trying to convey to the person or the group that you're talking to. Before saying or doing anything, ask yourself some or all of these questions:

- What is it that you want to achieve?
- What's the objective of your discussion?
- What's the outcome that you're after?
- Have you been clear about your expectations?
- What kind of perception do you want to create?
- Have you given sufficient thought to your discussion, maybe even written down some talking points, rather than just winging the whole thing?
- Have you anticipated the other person's reaction to what you're about to say or do, and are you prepared to address his or her reactions?

- Are you really ready to accept the consequences of putting the other person into the red zone? Because there will be consequences and they are usually not that pleasant, nor are they of the productive kind.

Before you say or do anything, decide what zone you want your message to be in and understand what you will achieve. For example, you'll never inspire or motivate anyone in the red zone. Motivation and inspiration can only occur in the green zone, the only place where "hugs" exist and the only place where they can be given. That's a simple truth that will positively help you be a better manager, a better parent, and a better communicator.

Simple Truth Nine: Sizing

Another technique I've used over the years to help managers remember the impact they have on other people and, therefore, to be mindful of what they say or do, is called "sizing."

People are going to react to what you say or what you do. That's human nature, but so often, that simple truth is taken for granted. People say and do things without taking a second or two to consider the kind of impact they will have on the other person. Sizing is a concept that can help you raise your awareness of how your words and actions affect others, and it can help you improve your interactions with, and management of, other people. Sizing is simple to understand and even simpler to put into practice. There can only be three sizes:

Same—Smaller—Bigger

Let me quickly give you some examples of this. How do you think the following statements will make the other person feel?

"You're an idiot, you should know better than that."

"I am so proud of you and so happy to be on the same team."

"That is a very interesting point of view."

The first statement is a put-down—it will make the person feel "smaller." The second remark is a compliment and a major positive—it makes the person feel "bigger." The third comment is neither positive nor negative—it keeps the individual at the "same" size. Another way to look at this sizing concept is to recall some of the earlier points we've talked about:

Recognition, appreciation, validation, thank-you note = Bigger
Rejection, bullying, intimidation, put-downs, scolding = Smaller
Coaching, helping, developing, discussing, aligning = Same

If it helps you to remember it, think of sizing as being similar to the analogy of the traffic lights that we described in the previous section:

Red Light = Smaller Size
Yellow Light = Same Size
Green Light = Bigger Size

The concept of sizing is very simple to understand and, with a little thought before saying or doing something, it can be a very effective technique in dealing with other people. Here are some other examples for your consideration:

"I just love the way you work, you're so reliable." (green, bigger)

"You really don't know what you're doing, do you? It's ridiculous!" (red, smaller)

"Don't you get it? We've gone over this a thousand times. Have you lost it?" (red, smaller)

"You did a great job persuading the production department to do that." (green, bigger)

"Please tell your daughter that your boss wishes her well in her recital." (green, bigger)

"I'm sorry to say but the last quarter was not what we wanted it to be." (yellow, same)

"Keep working on that. I'm anxious to see what you come up with." (yellow, same)

Obviously, the prime objective is to keep others at the same size or to lift them up. Invariably I'm asked, "Why not size them down? They screwed up. They need to be reprimanded. They need to know they goofed, they made a mistake." My answer is simple. Most of us were raised and conditioned in that manner, "Make a mistake, you had to be punished; you had to feel pain."

But we have to ask ourselves, what do we hope to achieve by following that conditioning? I thought we were here to try to make things better, to be better managers, to be better parents, to be more productive, to inspire and motivate people to achieve a higher level of success, to make the bottom line better, and all the other "better" things we have a responsibility to try to do.

And please don't tell me, "That's just the way it is." I don't buy it. I really don't buy that we can't make things better, that we can't improve things, that we must continue doing damage to other human beings. And then we wonder why life is so screwed up, why things don't get done, why there are so many teenage suicides, and why "same-ol'-same-ol'" is accepted as a new standard of mediocrity. If each of us can't even attempt to make things better, then what the hell are we doing with our lives?

Do what you want to do. Do what you're comfortable doing. And if that means "nothing," no problem. Just do me and many others a great big favor: lower the volume of the complaints so that those of us who want to can get on with making things better. And to those who are making things better, thanks a lot for doing that, it's much appreciated.

If that's too philosophical for some, let me give you a far more practical reason for not sizing others down, for not making them feel small. Think about this: the people you "size down" are the same people you will rely on to fix the problem, to find a solution, to clean up their room, to stop taking drugs, to stop drinking, to get on with their studies, to make something of themselves, and so on.

How are they supposed to do any of that when they have been cast into the "Shutdown Zone" where they become totally ineffective and go through the various reactions we described earlier? What kind of quality work do you think you're going to get? What kind of respect will they be able to give you? Perhaps most important of all, they learn nothing. They are not inspired to make improvements or to modify their ways. That's the simple truth of human behavior.

So in building relationships, in people management, in parenting, and in other interactions with people, please think, absorb, assimilate, digest, and apply both the Sizing and the Traffic Light principles. They really work—and they will help you become a better manager, a better parent, and a better you.

Now, let's get into a topic that has to do with you, rather than with how you deal with and manage others.

12

MANAGE HOW OTHERS PERCEIVE YOU

What is this and why do it? Great questions, the answers to which will heighten the importance of this topic. In fact, if there is a chapter that I suggest you read several times, it is this one. I say that because what follows is directed specifically at you, and how you manage yourself rather than managing others, which is what we've focused on so far.

It's designed to give you the power to understand, to control, and to enhance your future, whatever you decide that future may be. I want to help you derive greater satisfaction from both your work and your personal life. I also hope and pray that it will inspire you and give you the strength and confidence to reach your full potential as a human being. And before you read another word, let me quickly assert that all of the above is very possible, as evidenced by the hundreds of people I've coached in my career.

Let's start answering those questions. Managing how others see you, what they think about you, what they say about you, is vitally important to your career growth, to your development, and to your success in the corporate world, in your community, and everywhere else you interact with people. Therefore, it is absolutely vital that you make the time and put in the effort to manage and control how others perceive you. I call that "perception management."

The first important point is to understand that everything you say and everything you do will create the perception that people will have of you. Thus, you have the power to control how others perceive you. The next step is to decide what kind of perception you want to create. That's the hard part. It's your decision, so invest the time to do it well. It will help you to think of the following basic questions:

- What do you want others to say about you? If you were writing the script for them, what would the content be, what attributes would they confer upon you, and would they speak with a smile or a frown?
- What kind of lasting impression, or legacy, do you want to leave for others to remember you by?
- If you're into branding, what do you want your personal brand to be?

Once these questions are answered, you will have a personal strategy that should direct and guide what you say and do. That's powerful. Perhaps it will help you to think about perception management this way: As a manager, you may as well be seen as a positive individual who pays attention to people and recognizes and appreciates them, because if you're not—if you hurt and demean them instead—all of that will reflect back on you and the kind of person you are.

A positive perception is vital to your career advancement. If you simply can't get your head around doing the right thing for others, then do it for the sake of creating a positive impression of yourself. It never pays to be perceived negatively.

So how do you go about managing this perception thing? What do you have to be aware of? It's all about others, your employees, your family, your friends, and how you interact with them, how you treat them, what you allow them to learn about you, how you talk to them, how you behave toward them, how you react to the daily happenings of life, how you deal with challenges, how you manage success, and your overall demeanor. In other words, everything you say and everything you do will create the perception that others have of you.

I also want to point out that it's perfectly okay that the perception of you at work be different than the perception that people in your community will have of you, as it will be different from the one that your family has of you, and so on.

So let's consider some of the key elements that need to be seriously considered as you go about creating the perception that you want others to have of you. The perception of the "overall you," so to speak, will be based on how well you demonstrate some or all of the following:

- your skills and talents
- your personality
- your character
- your achievements
- your point of view
- your beliefs and principles
- your treatment of others
- your degree of professionalism
- your honesty and integrity
- your behavior toward others
- your attitude and how you express it
- your contributions to the business, to the community
- your spirit of generosity

The perception of you in the work environment will be determined by how well you conduct yourself in the various interactions you have with your people, with other departments, with senior management, with suppliers, and with your customers, be they external or internal ones. By way of example, and to get you engaged in this discussion, what kind of perception do you think will be created by the following actions and behaviors?

- The person who goes to a meeting and says nothing.
- The person who is heard yelling and screaming at someone.
- The person who stays late to get the job done.
- The person who is always late to various functions.
- The person who offers help to their colleagues.
- The person who seems always to complain about something.
- The person who always has something nice to say.
- The person who always has business-building ideas.

Here are some other "how-to" behaviors for you to put into practice in order for others to perceive you in a positive light:

- Make sure others see someone who is enthusiastic, positive, passionate, and excited about what they do.
- To be perceived as a leader, you need to come across as being helpful, a team player, willing to share ideas and be a very effective communicator.
- Ensure that you don't come across as one who's just in it for yourself, selfish, narcissistic.
- Never manage in the style of a tyrant, a dictator, a bully, or a yell-and-scream type.
- Always take responsibility for your actions, never blaming others for mistakes or finger-pointing at other departments to justify poor performance.

There are many other actions and behaviors that will dictate what kind of perception others will have of you, so please realize that whatever you say or do will create a perception. It's your decision whether that perception will be positive or negative, and also understand that you'll have to live with the consequences of that decision. What I mean by that is best illustrated by an actual incident that shook me to my core.

As Vice President of Marketing, Rose was charged with the responsibility of delivering the opening address at the national business meeting. An audience of 350 people awaited her remarks. She took the stage with a big round of applause; she was a popular VP, people liked her.

She started with the usual, "Good morning everyone, I'm delighted to see all of you," and so on. And then, for some inexplicable reason, began to tell a rather crude joke about sexual fantasies. The story had nothing to do with the business. She just wanted the attention of the audience, I guess.

What kind of perception did she create? What did people think of her? Did she demonstrate leadership, or anything close to it? The sad fact is that she was fired a few weeks later. Tragic. What a shame. What a waste of a truly talented individual, because of the poor perception she created in a very public forum.

Rose had all the skills and talents of a marketing guru, well regarded by her people and very well respected in the health and beauty industry. That was all thrown away by her decision to tell the joke. She certainly wasn't thinking about perception. To complete this true story, you should know that she fell into a deep depression. Don't do what Rose did. Her career came to an abrupt end.

This thing I've called "perception management," or managing how others perceive you, is very powerful stuff—powerful because it has a direct impact on your growth and development in both the workplace and in your personal life. You have full and complete control of it. So before you say or do anything, please take a minute to think about the kind of perception you are about to create.

As a way of summarizing the major points, here's a guidebook you should follow.

The Perception Management Guidebook

The pointers that follow may seem like common sense in creating and maintaining a positive perception for yourself in the workplace; however, we all know that common sense is not that common.

- Good performance on its own is important. But no matter how good you are at what you do, you have to ensure that the perception that others have of you is positive in both the technical aspects of the job and the interpersonal ones as well.
- Don't assume that time will heal mistakes or misdeeds. The only thing that time does is pass—from one second to the next.
- Do status reports on a monthly or quarterly basis to keep your bosses informed of the progress being made in your department.
- Make sure that you recognize the people in your area and in the other departments you deal with who deserve a round of applause.
- Write thank-you cards to people, colleagues and peers and, yes, to those in upper management. Of course, base the thanks on genuine actions they were helpful with.
- Strive to be different, to be special, and to have a grand-slam kind of business-building idea that generates incremental business.

- Create a major positive impact on the business that demonstrates your abilities, your creativity, your courage, your determination.
- Ensure that you take the time and make the effort to inspire and enliven your people. Say or do something that will make them proud to work with you.
- Make a promise—fulfill that promise.
- Be totally reliable—always achieve the goals set.
- Be a solution provider, not a complainer. Your bosses want to know exactly how you plan to resolve issues.
- Strive to be perceived as the go-to person.
- Operate and manage with total integrity.
- Always be on time for meetings and other events.
- Do not get drunk or be loud at company functions.
- Do not have affairs with employees.
- Always be appropriately dressed and groomed.
- Always go to meetings prepared to contribute positive comments.
- Don't steal the ideas of others and claim they are yours.
- Be generous with your time and efforts for others.
- Be helpful to others, be compassionate, be kind.
- Make sure your language is professional.
- Take initiatives to demonstrate your engagement.
- Demonstrate a positive attitude.
- Always achieve the goals set.
- Make recognition an integral part of your interactions with others.

Aside from all of these tips, please do not make the following assumption:

"I just assumed that my hard work and good results would speak for themselves."

In the business world, upper management wants and needs to know how things are going. They need to be reassured that the business is in capable hands; that progress is being made; that problems and roadblocks are being properly managed; that there is a sense of urgency; that people are accountable for what is happening in their area of responsibility.

If your career is important to you, you have to constantly manage the perception that you're creating for yourself, every single day in every single interaction you have with others. Look at it this way. You want to make sure that your star is shining brightly, not only in the eyes of upper management, but also in the eyes of your peers and the people you interact with.

For example, in the business world, meetings are an excellent way of creating the kind of perception that others will have of you. Here are some "how-to" things that you can employ immediately to create the positive perception you want others to have of you.

- Be an active and positive participant at the next meeting you attend. It will create a positive perception of you. On the other hand, if you object to everything and just complain about things you'll definitely create a perception—people will have no choice but to say you're a negative person.
- Be perceived as a solution-provider, as the go-to person who solves problems, by going to the meeting prepared to present well thought-out solutions that are best for the company, best for the team, and best for the people. You'll be seen as a thoughtful solution-provider.
- Show your appreciative side (and give deserving others a "hug") by praising and acknowledging the achievements of your people and the positive contributions of people in other departments. You'll be seen as a team player and not as some egotistical jerk who wants all the credit for himself.
- If there's a tough situation on the agenda, be prepared to accept responsibility for it if it falls under your leadership. Don't pass the buck, and don't point your finger at others. Blaming others creates a terrible perception. Be responsible. Be accountable. Offer solutions. Be prepared to say what you're going to do about the situation and how you'll resolve the matter in a timely and responsible manner. You'll be seen as a strong leader.

As a matter of fact, you should never attend a meeting (and heaven knows that's where a lot of your time is spent) without a deliberate plan to create a positive perception of yourself. Don't just sit there, as many do, doodling. Say or do something that creates a positive impact on the people that are in the meeting with you.

Another area that affords you the opportunity to create a positive perception is in the day-to-day interaction you have with others and the way you treat other people. From the minute you enter your office, you will create the perception that others will have of you as you go about doing your business. Here are some questions you should ask yourself.

- Do you greet all the people you see upon entering the office?
- Do you take a minute or so to say a kind word to someone?
- Do you just walk by everyone and not say a word?
- Do you say "please" and "thank you" to employees—in person and in emails?
- Is the tone of your voice friendly?
- Is the look on your face pleasant?
- Do you convey the fact that you are easy to approach?
- Do you use positive adjectives in what you write?
- Are you the "me-me" type in meetings or do you make the effort to recognize the other people in your department?
- Do you finger-point when things go wrong?
- Do you ever buy donuts for your team?
- What about donuts for the other teams who help your department?
- Do you write thank-you notes on a regular basis?
- Are you an open or closed person?
- Do you encourage others to submit ideas and suggestions?
- When the proverbial fan starts turning, do you yell and scream at others?
- Do you fly off the handle and lose your cool?
- Do others seek your advice and wisdom?
- Is recognition part of your daily, weekly, monthly routine?

The answers to these questions, and many others, are clear indications of the perception that you have the power to create for yourself. And when you think about it, it's relatively easy to do when you first determine what kind of perception you want others to have of you. That determination is the hard part. It's your decision and it's one that will actually liberate you by giving you direction and a strategy for your life and for how you will manage your behavior.

If your contemplated action fits the strategy—do it
If what you are thinking of saying or doing doesn't fit—don't do it

---

The final point I want to make about this crucial topic is this: How you treat people, be it at work, at home, wherever, is the major factor in how you will be perceived. Reject others, and you'll create a negative perception of yourself. Give others a "hug," metaphorically or physically, and you'll create a very positive perception.

A person can kill the positive perception others have of them in just one or two actions—and be labelled with whatever negative perception he or she has newly created—for a very long time. Pay attention to perception management every single day of your life—and remember, it's easy to create a great perception but much more difficult to rebuild or rekindle a poor perception. You'll enjoy life and be far more successful in what you do when the perception that others have of you is positive.

As an aside, my personal strategy—my legacy, my purpose—the perception I want people to have of me is very clear: "George helped me." I exist to help others. I want to make a difference in people's lives. I want to bring out the best in them and help them realize that they are more than they think they are. I want them to achieve more, to be more, and to enjoy more. I also want them to realize that they are better than they think, or have been told they are—better in the work they do, better in the interactions with their families, with their children, and even with themselves. That's the perception I have worked on creating all my life.

So, take time to think about the perception you want to create, shape it, give it dimension, check it out with a loved one, and then start giving life to it. Executing that perception then becomes relatively easy because you now have focus; you know what it is that you want to create. All you have to do is to look for the opportunities to do that, and if you can't find them, go out and create them.

Remember what George Bernard Shaw wrote in one of his plays, *Mrs. Warren's Profession*:

> *People are always blaming their circumstances for what they are.*
>
> *I don't believe in circumstances.*
>
> *The people who get on in this world are those who get up and look for the circumstances they need.*
>
> *And if they can't find them—they create them.*

13

FINDING THE BALANCE BETWEEN RIGHT AND WRONG

If there is a "disease" common to all people, it's our natural tendency to see every action as right or wrong. We all seem to be conditioned to see things as either right or wrong from the very beginning of our lives. We grow up with these guidelines and polar opposites firmly implanted in our minds.

Perhaps it's normal. Most, if not all, people are conditioned in the same way: things are right, or things are wrong. However, what is of concern to me is that we seem to be obsessed more with the wrong aspect than we are with the right. That smells like a disease to me. I refer to it that way primarily because I have experienced the harm and damage that focusing almost exclusively on the wrong, or the negative, causes so many people—be it in business, with family or just plain daily life.

There just doesn't seem to be a middle ground. You come home with a 76 score on one of your school subjects and you're made to feel like you did something wrong. The focus isn't on the fact that you were 76 percent right; the focus was on the 24 percent that you got wrong.

The other "disease" aspect of this conditioning is that a lot of parents use the right vs. wrong dichotomy as a basis for dishing out their affection, attention and recognition. Not all of them, but a majority of them do that, perhaps unknowingly, but they do. Unless you get things "right," all the good stuff like acceptance and validation, is withheld. For some parents, punishment is their preferred course of action.

No doubt, most parents want to raise their children knowing right from wrong. It's a great objective so I'm not arguing against it. What bugs me is the lack of balance between positive and negative. There's way too much focus on the things that are wrong rather than on the things that are right. There's too much emphasis on the negative rather than on the positive, and we all know by now how damaging that can be to a person's psyche.

In the world of business, it's no different, unfortunately. Too many managers seem to spend all their time and energy watching for their employees to do something wrong, rather than trying to catch them doing something right.

The vital message here is to avoid a negative approach because you're focused on the "wrong" aspects. "Wrong" puts people on the defensive, 24/7—and the opportunity to coach is lost, period. Rather than taking advantage of a coaching moment, which allows you to recognize and praise the individual for the "right" things he or she has done, you end up rejecting the person by picking on the "wrong" things they did.

With parents, teachers, and bosses alike, there most often doesn't appear to be any tolerance or acceptance of anything else but right and wrong, or even an understanding that there just might be a middle zone between these two opposites. The prime reason for that is that people don't take the time to ask 1,001 questions to see and to understand the other person's perspective, his idea, his approach to things, and perhaps to discover a better way. Rather, we are quick to evaluate an individual's performance with that "right vs. wrong" thinking. We're constantly on watch for, and quick to point out, "That's wrong!"

Because of that, we ourselves are on edge, aware that we'll be judged in the same manner as we judge others, on the basis of "right vs. wrong." This only serves to accentuate the fear of failure, in ourselves and in others. We're afraid to do something wrong and those we have a relationship with are equally afraid to do something wrong. That's not a healthy situation for anyone. This fear of being wrong, of failing, of being rejected, is a powerful negative force, and the number-one fear in the world. It beats the fear of snakes, spiders, flying, and yes, even the fear of dying.

People are so afraid to be wrong. They are so afraid to make a mistake that they often just shut down. It's highly unlikely that they will ever take risks, ever venture out to try something different. I know people who are afraid to drive a car because they are afraid they might get into an accident. This fear hampers their progress, their growth and, yes, their own health. Years later they wonder why their careers stalled, why they didn't realize their dreams—and why they feel so empty deep inside, where it counts the most.

If you're a manager and are wondering why your employees don't come up with new, fresh ideas to improve the business, it's probably because they are afraid of being wrong, of being rejected. Have you ever considered how your own behavior may be influencing your employees in this way? Have you ever thought about the fact that your own persistent negativity might have such negative consequences for someone else, or that you can turn all that around by giving more positive feedback?

If you're a manager of people and wonder why your people are not creative, not risk takers, not quick to make decisions, in fact, hesitate to make decisions, guess what—they're afraid of being wrong, of being rejected. They shut down so you're left with having to make the decisions. You thus tend not to engage them in the process, which negatively impacts the trust you have in them.

If you're a manager of people, please understand that your people may still be hearing the voices of their past, not just yours, "Don't do this, don't do that; that's wrong; you're always screwing things up; you keep making the same mistakes over and over; how many times have I told you not to do that, not to say that," and on and on and on with the baggage they carry from earlier times.

The fact is, we all have baggage and bring it into our work and into every relationship we have. And here's the "watch out," the words of caution for you: every time we are told we are wrong, the voices of the past rise up and begin their chorus of debilitation. Whatever the exact phrases were that we heard as children, they linger on, they never stop, never to be erased on the hard-drive of our minds. These are the "hurt files" we talked about earlier.

So what do we do? After all, there are right and wrong situations that we have to face every day of our lives. Life is not all sweet and roses and wonderful. Stuff happens. We all make mistakes. We all do right and we all do wrong. Well, there are two answers to the question of how to manage this.

- The first answer is contained in the how-to arena of dealing with the mistakes, dealing with those things that are wrong. Simply stated, you have a choice to make as a manager, as a parent, as a spouse, or as a friend. You can attack the person, or you can attack the problem.
- I'm going to assume that you know what the "right" answer is on this issue, but just in case: attack the problem, never the person, as we mentioned earlier.
- The second answer is to recognize that there is a middle zone between the right and wrong ones. I call it wisdom.

| RIGHT | WISDOM | WRONG |

- I like the word "wisdom" because it encompasses so much: understanding, knowledge, insight, perception, astuteness, and intelligence. That's a lot of great stuff wrapped up in a single word, and it's all positive.
- Wisdom opens things up, so to speak. It allows an individual to gain knowledge, to acquire insight into a subject and to gain overall intelligence. I also like the word "wisdom" because it describes the essence of learning: trying to do things, experimenting, taking risks, searching for answers, and just going for it.

Ask yourself, isn't the mere act of trying something new or different of great value? Where would we be if Alexander Graham Bell hadn't tried and failed so many times before he figured out that thing we call a telephone?

For a manager of people, that means that he or she needs to focus on the wisdom/learning aspect of people's actions, even when a mistake is made. Rather than the usual "it's wrong" approach accompanied by a put-down of the person, the "wisdom" approach is all about asking questions such as:

- What did we learn from that?
- How will this learning be applied to future actions?
- How will this help to make us better?
- How will this help us to become more efficient, more effective, and more profitable?

We talked about the immense benefits of using the 1,001 questions technique in an earlier chapter. That's such a vital approach to use, especially in this "right or wrong" discussion. I made the point earlier that people know when they've made a mistake, when they missed the objective, when their arrow misses the bulls eye, when they don't get 100 percent on the exam, and when things don't work out the way they hoped they would. So I have to ask, "What's the point of blaming the individual and jamming their failure down their throat? Please tell me what you'll achieve by that."

Please ask yourself what is achieved by reinforcing the "wrong," "I already feel bad. Why does he put me down to make it worse for me? How am I supposed to recover from being rejected?" The answer is that nothing, absolutely nothing, will be achieved by focusing only on what has gone wrong, except to create a very depressed and unmotivated individual, not to mention the poor perception you'll create of yourself.

The easy solution is to seek and gain wisdom about the situation and, together, move forward with that wisdom to make things better in the future. And the only way to achieve that is by putting your blame finger away and get into the habit of asking 1,001 wisdom-seeking questions. They will force the other person to think. That will enable you to really know what the strengths of the individual are; the quality of his thinking; the sense of urgency he displays; the remorse he shows, if that's called for; and his passion to be better and to be successful. The 1,001 questions technique works—it's fact-finding at its best. Even more important, there's no need to use your blame-finger.

That's a very different, and far more positive, approach than the one we've been conditioned to use. Let's remember that each mistake can lead us to greater success, if the mistake is viewed as an opportunity for learning, or to gain wisdom. If we make a mistake and we learn from it, we acquire wisdom, knowledge and experience—and that is very positive. It's the central key to progress. It's virtually the only way of making things better.

A Balanced Approach

Unfortunately, wisdom, in all of its aspects, does not always prevail. When people are focused on what the other person does wrong, then we have a major problem in the way we live and the way we manage others. Please consider this. How can anyone function and give their best when they are under the microscope, constantly being scrutinized and monitored for every action they take and every word they speak?

I know what you're thinking right about now, "Isn't it important to point out the negatives, the mistakes and the failures of others? How else do people learn? How else do they get to know what is right?" Great questions. Good on you for asking them. And I'm not about to argue with you. What I'm putting on the table for your consideration is the importance, actually vital importance, to have a balanced approach in your interactions with others.

If you want to look for the "wrong" things the other person does, fine, do so. But—and it's a big but—make sure you spend as much time and effort (preferably more) looking for, seeking out, and making note of all the "right" things the other person is doing as well.

Have a balanced approach—that's the "wisdom" approach.

I say that because a focus on "wrong" harms the other person. It creates a "hurt file" that will be with the individual for the rest of his life. That's what happens when there isn't a balanced approach, the "wisdom" approach. Maybe I'm crazy to think that that can change, but I do believe that we can modify our behaviors and actions if we understand that there is another view on this "right versus wrong" thinking. So before you think I'm crazy, please do the following: Take a piece of blank paper and draw two circles several inches apart. Let's call the two circles "right" and "wrong." Between right and wrong, write the word, wisdom.

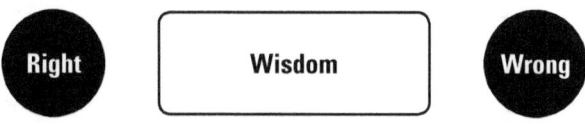

Now that you have a visual, let me ask:

- Do we learn when we do things right? Of course we do.
- Do we learn when we do things wrong? Of course we do.

So in fact, right and wrong have a common element. They are both the source of learning, of knowledge, and hence of wisdom. Yet wisdom is not what our parents focused on. It is not what our schools focus on. It is not what our bosses focus on. It is not what we focus on with our families. Please remember:

We all learn and gain wisdom from doing things right.

We all learn and gain wisdom from doing things wrong.

Instead of, "Go to your room and stay there until I tell you to come out," how about something along the lines of:

"Please come over here and let's see what we learned from what just happened."

"How can we apply what we learned from that incident and use the skills you have to ensure it doesn't happen again?"

"I really admire your courage for trying that. It didn't work out as planned but that's life. The key now is to examine what we learned and then course-correct so that we meet the objectives before us and don't repeat the same errors."

These are slightly different from the usual "blast of temper" aren't they? The last example above also shows that even when we do have to point out a mistake or something that was done wrong, we can easily add a positive note into the mix. It's as much how we say what we are communicating as it is what we actually say. In other words, even if you have to criticize, correct, or point out a mistake, it's important to start off by finding something positive to point out. Then the rest of your feedback will be more willingly received, and it will be far less hurtful. Notice that in the last example above, the speaker offers up some positive feedback first, some encouragement, before going on to discuss the actual error in question.

What's fascinating to me is that we don't need to take special courses to understand and apply this wisdom approach. We do it already. We already have that capability. We already know when to zip it up and say nothing. The fact is that over the years, we've learned to say or do things that we know are wise, even though we know that the other person has made a mistake. We zip it up because we have learned that very often wisdom must prevail, and that it's the best approach under the circumstances. Here's a real example, to prove the point.

You're sitting down for dinner with the family. The conversation is great, the kids are laughing, sharing fun stories about their day at school, and so on. It's all good. Then you bite into the chicken dinner. Ooops. You can't help but notice that there's too much salt. If we were to do a lab test, you'd be right, the salt content exceeds the recommended daily dose of some agency, and certainly exceeds what your palate likes. So, the lab test and your palate both prove that you're right—too much salt! Now the dirty questions:

- Do you blurt out the fact that there's too much salt, thus being critical?
- What exactly do you hope to achieve, what is your purpose in saying anything?
- Do you think it's wise to point out that there is something wrong with your partner's cooking?
- What does anyone learn from your focus on what's wrong?
- Will you feel good about completely wiping out the good time everyone is having?
- Is your being right more important than family harmony?

And, by the way, don't you think everyone else, including the cook, will notice that there is too much salt, and possibly laugh at it? Why reinforce the obvious and be hurtful? Focusing on what's wrong is not a wise approach in this situation. It serves no purpose. Have another drink of water, you'll be fine, and tell everyone around the table that you love these family dinners.

In the business environment this sort of situation happens almost every day, usually during a meeting:

> "Before we move on to the next topic, I want you all to know how disappointed I am at losing the order that George said he would get. It shouldn't have happened. I've said a thousand times, 'Make a promise, deliver that promise.' That did not happen, George.
>
> "And now the entire department is impacted by your actions and how you went about dealing with the customer. It was wrong from start to finish. And what really ticks me off is that when I asked if you needed help, your answer was a blunt, 'I know what I'm doing.' You were wrong, you didn't know what you were doing. And now all of us are saddled with the problem you've created."

We could ask the same questions as we did with the "too much salt" issue. In many situations, and in a variety of circumstances, we need to understand and be comforted by the fact that in between right and wrong lies the valuable and most beneficial aspects of wisdom.

That understanding should open up the tolerance levels we have of our employees, our friends and of course, our families. That understanding should also greatly reduce, if not greatly minimize, what seems to be an insatiable desire to focus on the "wrong" that hurts people and shuts them down.

It really serves no purpose to do that, and, even more important, it takes away the opportunity to encourage, to support, to learn, to experience, and to develop new ways, better ways, of dealing with things.

Focusing on "wrong" is backward-thinking
Focusing on "wisdom" is forward-thinking

So, you have a choice to make as a manager, as a parent, as a spouse, or as a friend. Please remember and employ the principles we talked about earlier:

Don't Punish, Coach
Attack the problem, never the person
Use the Wisdom Approach

And if all that is still not convincing you, let me give you another real example. One of the most compelling examples of the power of this wisdom approach comes from the world of baseball. I'm sure you know that Babe Ruth earned the title of Home Run King because of the 714 home runs he hit during his career (without steroids, I might add). But did you know that Babe Ruth held another baseball record? He was also the Strikeout King. Imagine, two amazing records held by the same person: the Home Run King (right) and the Strikeout King (wrong).

When Babe Ruth was asked how he felt about his strikeouts, he simply replied, "Every time I struck out, I knew that I was closer to hitting a homerun." He did not see striking out as a failure but rather as a step closer to success and achievement. His "wrong" was getting him closer to being "right." What a superb attitude, one that we should all learn and gain wisdom from!

The fascinating thing is that Babe Ruth was motivated and inspired by what many people would have considered to be the wrong action. Again, let me ask you, if you were Babe's manager, would you have berated him, scolded him, maybe even fired him (traded him) for striking out so many times? So why do you get so impatient with your staff? Why do you "let 'em have it" when they do something you perceive to be wrong? Do you ever consider instead that their effort will be a learning experience, one that will bring them much closer to success and achievement?

I trust that makes the vital point that one of the prime responsibilities of a manager—and one of the key ways of managing people, both at work and in your personal life—is to minimize the focus on what's wrong and use the balanced wisdom approach.

As best you can, you want to remove the fear of making a mistake. Mistakes will be made. The sign of a great leader is how they manage the people who make the mistakes, and how they manage themselves throughout the process.

It's not a mistake—it's learning

It's not a mistake—it's experience

It's not a mistake—it's one step closer to success

It's not a mistake—it's gaining wisdom

Here's a chart that may help put this entire discussion into perspective:

The "Wrong" Approach	The "Wisdom" Approach
Usual questions = What happened? Who did it?	*New Question = How can <u>we</u> resolve this?*
This approach tends to blame, perhaps attack, express anger, verbal abuse of others usually happens.	The objective here is to get to the solution quickly with a "we" spirit, and a positive sense of teamwork.
Reprimand heightens fear, anxiety, stress, and intensifies the sense of rejection and failure.	The focus is on resolving the issue, not on reprimanding the person or the people, verbal abuse is out of the equation.
Rejection debilitates and diminishes the talents, the skills, even the value of others; it "sizes" the other person down, makes them feel smaller, incapable, not good enough.	This encourages solutions by using the talents and skills of the people to resolve the situation; we can actually "size" the person up. The solution is usually quicker, more effective.
Confidence is shaken, individual is traumatized, causing "shutdown." The individual being sized down is not motivated to work toward a solution.	This approach is a confidence builder. People are given the opportunity to resolve things and to accomplish something; it even encourages learning.
With confidence reduced, we shut off creativity, knowledge, and the motivation to resolve the situation.	Confidence opens the door to creativity, to ideas and to suggestions that address the matter in a positive way.
We're now faced with having to manage a stressed, disgruntled, mistrusting, de-motivated employee.	This approach actually provides an opportunity to say thanks and show appreciation, and thus motivate the individual.

As I'm sure you noticed, there's a big difference between the two approaches. So why is it that most of us use the "wrong" approach? To repeat, I believe it's simply a matter of conditioning. We are conditioned, as we grow up, to see the world through only two lenses: right and wrong. Now you have another lens to look through: the wisdom lens. And that gives you the opportunity to turn just about every mistake or negative event into something positive, into a coaching and a learning moment.

14

THE PERFECTIONIST'S PRISON

Earlier in this book, we've already seen how fundamentally we all want to please others—our parents, teachers, managers—because that will give us the positive attention and recognition we crave. Well, perfectionists take that impulse to a whole new level. They strive not only to please others, but to be perfect in everything they do. Their fear of failure is off the charts, and one of their primary drivers.

Right off the top, let me say that perfectionists are the most difficult and the most challenging people to coach. They can also be among the most difficult to work for, and the most difficult to manage. Perfection is an impossibly high standard to live up to and, therefore, perfectionists can be some of the most frustrating, frustrated, and most unhappy people to deal with.

At the same time, they are the most rewarding to coach and to help, because once the chains of being a perfectionist are removed, the individual soars to new heights of achievement. They are freed from the stresses and the frustrations they have lived with for so long. They are liberated. They start doing things they never thought possible because of the new-found courage they have. Their self-esteem, which has been "sized down" for so long, finally shoots up and they experience an entirely new sense of fulfillment and satisfaction. In so many ways, they become a new person.

That has to be the most rewarding gift a coach can ever help another person to acquire. And I say that because solving a problem is one level of satisfaction, but giving another human being a lifetime gift takes that satisfaction to a new and heightened level. So let's get into this fascinating topic.

The World Needs Perfectionists, But…

In principle, there's nothing wrong with being a perfectionist, nothing wrong with wanting to do things perfectly. That's an admirable aim. In fact, the world needs perfectionists:

- I want the airline pilot to make a perfect landing.
- I want the architect to make sure the drawings for the building are perfect.
- I want the contractor to ensure that all the pieces fit perfectly.
- I want the accountant to make sure the books are perfect.
- I want the heart surgeon to make a perfect incision.
- I want the engineer to make sure the bridge is perfect.

I want perfectionists in the world. Some tasks and some jobs demand perfection, and there's nothing wrong with that. But true perfectionists take that too far and seek to be perfect in everything they do. They drive themselves and others crazy trying to live up to, and hold others to, an impossibly high standard. However, what bothers me is the harmful toll they have to pay for being a perfectionist:

- stress, frustration, anxiety
- never being pleased with what they do
- not being able to make decisions because of the fear of failure
- not trusting others to do what they've asked them to do
- always correcting others for what they've done
- being a "doer" rather than a leader
- being their own worst enemy
- limiting the ability to reach their full potential
- limiting creativity, initiatives, risk-taking
- limiting their ability to live a full and complete life

You're right, not every perfectionist suffers from all of the above; but the point is that any one of the above is a huge toll to pay, and it inevitably leads to all kinds of mental and medical problems. That, in essence, is what bothers me about perfectionists. Their search for attention and appreciation is enviable on the one hand, but, frankly, a foolish quest that is fraught with so much pain and hurt. Sadly, they don't realize that. Many live a life unfulfilled, unsatisfied. They just go on driving themselves harder and harder in the hope that, by being perfect in all that they do, they'll finally get the accolades they've always wanted.

What is also very tragic is the fact that if they manage people, they push these people to the brink of frustration. They are never pleased with what their employees do; they tend to be micro-managers, not trusting anyone. Frankly, they drive their people crazy. And, here's the big punch line: they are virtually incapable of expressing appreciation for the good work their employees generate. The fact is, most people hate to work for them. The stress and frustration employees feel by being pushed to achieve perfection in everything they do is simply too great and too hurtful—and for many, too debilitating.

If you are a perfectionist, work for one, manage one, live with one, then you need some strategies to manage work and life effectively. The irony is that most perfectionists are driven by a powerful fear of failure, but striving for perfection in fact sets them up to fail. Humans are not built to be perfect, at least not all the time.

The Making of a Perfectionist

Perfectionists are created just the same way as you, me, and anybody else walking about in this world. They are shaped by the same two fundamental forces—recognition and rejection—that we've learned and read about at length earlier in this book. They just seem to be more sensitive to rejection and hurt than some other people, and take their reaction to it to further lengths than most. Sadly, some perfectionists may also have had to endure more hurt in the formative years than the rest of us.

Here are some of the things I've heard from perfectionists in so many coaching sessions over the years:

"No matter what I did, they were never pleased. They were always on me for something, no matter how good I was in the eyes of others."

"I'm leaving home because my father doesn't want me to take an arts course. He thinks I should go into business, even though I hate it."

"My sister gets all the love because she's a straight A student. I just get grief from them because I'm more into sports than into the books."

"I just wonder if they'll ever be pleased with me."

"I'm the CEO of the company and my father still hasn't told me he's proud of me. Yes, it hurts like hell."

"No matter what I did as a child, no matter what I do today, they're never happy with me, never pleased, never satisfied, never told me I was good, never told me they were proud of me, never showed me real appreciation, never gave me the recognition I worked so hard to get from them."

"I guess I'll just have to do better, try harder, and try to be perfect. That must be the only way I will get their appreciation and acceptance."

"If I do this perfectly, they will finally appreciate me."

"Being perfect must be the only way to have them say I'm good."

I can't begin to count the number of men and women who have never felt the affection or appreciation of their parents, who have never heard phrases like, "I'm so proud of you."

These real expressions of hurt confirm what we have seen over and over again throughout the book. All a child wants from his or her parents is to be loved. That sounds obvious, and it is. Clearly, the comments above reveal a complete void of affection and appreciation in the lives of these people. That conditioning stays with the child, the person, for the rest of his or her life. The voices of the parents linger on, never to be forgotten—but forever to be heard almost every single day.

Again, perfectionists simply take all of this to the next level, feeling that they have no choice but to be perfect in everything they do, in order to avoid failure and to please others. There's just one major problem with that, and it's a question that every perfectionist wrestles with: "Which definition of perfect will please others and enable them to give me the appreciation I need to sustain my life?" The search for that definition of "perfect" becomes life's work for so many people. Hence the perfectionist is born.

The Price of Perfection

Is the price for being a perfectionist really worth it? I'll try to answer that question and, in so doing, try to relieve the stress and frustration that you perfectionists out there—and those who have to live with them, work with them, and deal with them—are no doubt enduring.

First, I want you to accept the fact that you're a perfectionist. There's nothing inherently wrong with that, so don't think of it as being a bad thing or that something is wrong with you. You're great the way you are, okay?

Second, I want you to consider and evaluate the amount of stress you have in your life. Use a 1 to 10 scale, 10 being very high. Then I want you to think about the various aspects of your life and score each one on the same scale. Here's an example of the kind of scale you can use to do this exercise.

Stress Scores

Job	1 _____	10
Kids	1 _____	10
Spouse	1 _____	10
Finances	1 _____	10
Friends	1 _____	10
Hobbies	1 _____	10
Education	1 _____	10

By all means, expand the list with as much detail as you'd like. Actually, the more the merrier, and the better you'll understand yourself. What we're trying to do here is get you to see that not everything you do has the same level of stress. I'm hoping that you'll have an assortment of scores: some fives, some sixes and, yes, probably a lot of tens. That's okay. Now you know yourself much better in terms of those things that stress you out and those things that don't punish you as much.

Third, and this is a tough one to do, I want you to think about "the voices" you hear in your head and try to determine if they are at the same levels for each activity that you do. Do the voices subside from time to time or are they loud all the time? Look at the list you just did. Now score it from 1 to 10, based on the voices you hear for each topic.

Voices Score

Job	1 _____	10
Kids	1 _____	10
Spouse	1 _____	10
Finances	1 _____	10
Friends	1 _____	10
Hobbies	1 _____	10
Education	1 _____	10

So you'll have two sets of numbers: one set for stress levels and the other for voices.

Stress Scores   *Voices Scores*

The scores should be very different. Now we're cooking, because what this exercise will reveal to you is the fact that the voices drove you to perfection on some things, but not on all things.

The key understanding, I hope you see, is that in some areas you were driven to perfection by your parents. They pushed you to be better, to do better, and so on. Only you know exactly what they said to you, and only you know that they withheld their appreciation for you until you did exactly what they wanted. It was conditional love, wasn't it? What were you to do but to give in to it? A child has no other choice, "If you want a hug, then do what I tell you."

The next key learning from these exercises is to realize that you began your own conditioning program, so to speak. You pushed yourself to be a perfectionist in what you were doing and in how you lived, in how you conducted your relationships, in how you worked, in how you managed people, and in how you raised your children, and so on.

So here's the reality check that should help you manage things from now on. The voices of your parents cannot be erased or eliminated. Sorry about that, but that's the reality that you need to understand, even if you don't like it. But—and this is crucial—you can learn how to cope with, control, and modify your own voice, the one that is driving you to perfection today. Here's the technique I've recommended and used with great success with my clients.

Be a Selective Perfectionist: Not Everything Has to Be at a 10

To become a selective perfectionist requires a practical understanding of the fact that not all tasks require the same amount of energy and intensity. Not all tasks require the same amount of time and effort. Or, as I have often said to clients, "You don't have to go to 18 decimal places to achieve perfection when two will do."

In other words, the return on effort is just not the same for every task that you have to do. It's just not worth the enormous amounts of energy that you expend on everything. Being a selective perfectionist means learning how to focus on the objective of what it is you are trying to achieve, rather than getting mired in the details of how it is done.

After all, you're doing whatever you're doing for a reason, so what is that reason? And that has to be made clear well before starting any project, especially if you're going to involve someone else. It's the same principle as the concept of clarity of expectations that we talked about earlier. Here are some questions to ask yourself in trying to have clarity, even about things that involve only you:

- What is the objective?
- Is this the only way to achieve the objective?
- What is it that I'm trying to prove, and to whom?
- Is what I'm doing really worth the time and effort?
- Is there something more important for me to be doing?
- Will what I'm about to do help others, inspire others?
- Am I taxing myself needlessly—physically and mentally?
- Is this really worth the extra effort?
- Compared to other projects I have to do, where does this rank in order of importance?
- Will this help increase the sales and profits of the company?

Perfectionists don't usually go through these questions. To them every task is important. They can't seem to distinguish one from another.

They spend days preparing speeches and presentations. They make all kinds of slides to support their talk. They spend an inordinate amount of time and effort because they feel compelled to show the audience virtually everything they know about the subject. They don't want to fail or be rejected. So they think that by showing the audience everything about the subject, they can't possibly fail. The focus is on their perfectionist self, without regard for what their audience really needs to hear, or how their message will help the audience.

It is only after they give the presentation that they realize that their audience was bored out of their mind because the presentation did not address their needs. And even then, they usually won't admit it, and instead blame the audience for one thing or another. Why does this happen to perfectionists?

Perfectionists have a common thought process, and it usually goes like this: "In order for me to be recognized, I've got to show the audience that I am perfect. I have to show them that I know everything about the subject or it won't be good enough to win their approval. I can't live with myself if I do otherwise."

On the surface, that may sound reasonable to many ears. After all, it kind of makes sense that anybody would want to know as much about a subject as possible. The more knowledge one has the better. "Knowledge is power" is a saying that has been with us for ages, so it must be true. And it is. However, like many other things in life, there are degrees of knowledge, degrees of understanding, and certainly degrees of perfection.

The conditioning to be perfect in everything you do and everything you say is an unfair burden that you have carried on your shoulders for a long time. The voice that says, "It just isn't good enough," has to be quelled, once and for all. You have to free yourself of living with the fear of failure hanging over your every move, your every word. It's a fear that has serious consequences:

- I'm burnt out. I'm really tired. I have no more energy.
- I have no time to think, no time to be creative, no time to brainstorm ideas.
- I feel like all I do is spin my wheels, going nowhere.
- Many days I feel paralyzed, unable to solve problems or deal with issues.
- It's hard to work more than 15 hours a day, yet I have so much to do.
- Weekends? Forget it, I have to catch up. No time to fool around.
- I hate my job. All I do is tumble numbers and do PowerPoint presentations.

Those statements are tragic. They are the consequences of trying to be perfect in everything, all the time. They are the consequences of living under that fear of failure umbrella that invariably accompanies the quest to be perfect.

What I've tried to do in the last few pages is to offer tried-and-true exercises that will help you become a selective perfectionist. Let me be very clear about that: be a perfectionist, no problem. No one is going to change that basic element of your character—and, frankly, it can't be done. But you can train yourself to become a selective perfectionist and help yourself by learning how to recognize the most important tasks and objectives, prioritize them, and allocate your time and energy appropriately. You'll greatly improve your outlook and your interactions with others.

> **Benefits of Becoming a Selective Perfectionist**
>
> - It will loosen the shackles you've carried for so many years.
> - It will liberate you.
> - You'll have more time.
> - You'll be able to get the "hug" that you deserve.
> - You'll become more creative. You'll be able to lighten up.
> - You'll have more fun.
> - You'll be easier to get along with.
> - You won't be constantly punishing yourself.
> - You'll stop being your own worst enemy.
> - You'll actually achieve greater success.

Earlier, I suggested doing two exercises: develop a Stress Score and a Voices Score. Now let's address your to-do list of activities, one for your work life and one for your personal life.

Write down every task you have to do, in no particular order; just write down what comes to mind. Now give each item on that list a score from 1 to 10. Ten is the ultimate effort, the ultimate intensity that you will give to this task, the perfection you'll strive for! And remember, be a selective perfectionist, not every task deserves a 10! There's no right or wrong score. Just write down what comes to mind.

> *To-Do List*
>
> Score   1 _____ 10
>
> Marketing Plan   8
> Spouse Birthday   10
> Clean Basement   4
> Visit Aunt Mary   3
> Daughter's Ballet   9
> Pick up bagels   2

The point is to consider carefully what has to be done and the degree of perfection that item really requires. There has to be a fair degree of perfection allowed for some important, high-priority tasks or events—some items will get a 6, others have to be a 7 and, yes, indeed, some will deserve a 9, even a 10.

The key point is that not all tasks need to be done to the 10/10 degree of perfection. The irony is that you probably don't even know what a perfect 10 looks like for most things that you do. You just keep working crazy hours, not really knowing what success looks like, as one of my clients and friends would say. He's always asking his people that question and it's amazing what kind of answers he gets. So, let me borrow a page from his very successful management style, "What does 10 out of 10 look like for every item on your to-do list?"

- What does 10 out of 10 look like when it comes to renovating the kitchen?
- What does 10 out of 10 look like when it comes to celebrating your 40th anniversary?

And what does perfection look like at work? For example, I've worked with a lot of people who keep revising their PowerPoint slides, trying to make them "perfect," even though they really had no idea of what a perfect slide should look like.

How Do You Define Perfection?

Can anyone out there define what a perfect slide looks like?

Can anyone out there define what a perfect marketing plan looks like?

Can anyone out there define what a perfect sales call looks like?

Can anyone out there define what a perfect apple pie tastes like?

Does anyone out there have the perfect hamburger recipe?

How about the perfect paint color for the living room?

What's the perfect golf swing?

> How many decimal places do you really need before you convince yourself that the financial report is excellent?
>
> Are you sure you want to work on draft 12 of your speech? Is that the magic number that you'll be satisfied with, or will it be version 15?

I could go on and on with examples and questions about what "perfect" looks like, but I trust that you get the point, and that the 1 to 10 scale will enable you to carefully consider what has to be done and the degree of effort, energy, intensity and perfection that the item really deserves. If you strive for 10 out of 10 on everything, you won't have any time left or any energy left to do other things, such as:

- Time to think
- Time to be creative
- Time to embark on a new project
- Time to be a solution-provider
- Time to demonstrate the hidden skills and talents you have
- Time to be a leader
- Time to help others
- Time to build others up
- Time to be a great friend
- Time to be a great father/mother
- Time to look in the mirror and realize how spectacular you really are
- Time to accomplish more

Paradoxically, relaxing your tendency to be a perfectionist in everything will actually allow you to achieve more and to be better at more things. Instead of wasting energy on little things that don't deserve them, you'll be focusing your time and energy on the priorities that are truly important, and using your time and talents much more efficiently.

Accomplishing more will allow you to enjoy an entirely new and heightened level of satisfaction in your work life and, even more important, in your personal life. To use a common expression, dialing back your perfectionist tendencies will allow you to lighten up. The tasks of life will suddenly appear to be less onerous, more enjoyable and far more nourishing and satisfying.

Oh, and before I forget, becoming a selective perfectionist will also give you the crucial time needed for you to be kind and generous and wonderful and gracious to the most important person of all—YOU. Go on, give yourself a hug!

15

BE A LEADER—DEMONSTRATE LEADERSHIP

The distinction between being a leader and demonstrating true leadership is a very hot topic in every organization and one that is constantly being defined and redefined. It's one that I'm always asked about:

- Are people born leaders?
- Can you learn how to be a leader?
- Do you have to be a tough so-and-so to be a leader?
- What makes someone a good leader?
- What about leadership? How do you define that?
- What are the behavioral attributes of a leader?
- Does it take special skills to be a leader?
- Are there specific leadership courses?

These, and many others, are great questions. In my experience, I have yet to come across any definitive answers. It's as if everyone has their own definition and their own view on the topics of being a "leader" and "leadership."

Here's what we should be able to agree on. Poor leaders do a lot of damage to an organization—to its growth, to its potential, and to its people. A simple look around the business landscape will reveal numerous companies that have disappeared because of poor leaders and their poor leadership.

Conversely, good leaders help to build not only business results and their organizations, but also the people in them. They have qualities that enable them to bring out the best in people, to realize the full potential of their employees, and to create a culture of success. These qualities are often intangible, but there is no doubt they are critical and to be encouraged and developed. Strong leadership skills have to be a major consideration in the promotion or appointment of people into the role and responsibility of leader.

In my experience, there is a great distinction between the position of "leader" and the actions, behaviors and attributes of "leadership." Let's explore that distinction in some detail in order to understand fully the ramifications of leadership development for your own organization, and the consequences of the decisions you will have to make about the people in your business.

First, let me explain for you the important distinction between being a leader and exhibiting true leadership. In my experience with many clients over the years, these can be two very different things.

- **Leader:** By virtue of their title, a person may be in the position of "leader," the individual in charge, the boss, the chief, the director, the top banana. But that does not mean that he or she is capable of demonstrating true "leadership." Their title says "leader" but it does not automatically confer "leadership" qualities on them. A leader can be a leader in name only.
- **Leadership:** An individual may be a great leader even though he or she does not have the official title or position of "leader." He or she may demonstrate great leadership abilities and qualities regardless of their title. True leadership is exhibited and proven by someone's actions. There are many people who model leadership qualities without holding the position or title of "leader." True leadership can be shown by any employee, in any position, at any level in the organization.

Leadership, by definition, requires a keen understanding of human behavior and the art of balancing technical skills with people skills. Leadership, amongst many things, is the ability to inspire others, to bring out the best in others, and to help develop others to realize their full potential.

Organizations often make the mistake of putting people into leadership positions without asking whether or not they have true leadership skills. Too often, they seem to be in a hurry to give the job to a technically competent warm body, to appoint a leader without determining if that person has true leadership abilities. That is a huge mistake.

So what are the leadership skills you should look for and develop in your people, and maybe rekindle in your own management style and actions?

Demonstrate Leadership—Become a Leader

We've talked about many of the leadership skills earlier in the book, but they are worth reviewing again. In many ways, everything we've talked about so far has been to help make you a better leader. It's a long summary of what we've covered but I want to emphasize these points because of how helpful they will be to you.

- Make recognition your most powerful skill.
- Take rejection out of your lexicon, forget it.
- Create coaching moments and coach, never punish.
- Attack the issue, never the person.
- Never yell and scream—at the office, at home.
- Do not bully, intimidate, abuse, or harass.
- Inspire and motivate people.
- Make people feel "big;" never put people down.
- Develop a great balance between "head" and "heart."
- Forget the "wrong" style of management.
- Use "wisdom" as a learning and growth driver.
- Don't be a micro-manager.
- Make a decision on what has to be done.
- Clearly outline your expectations to your people.
- Align with your people on objectives, deadlines, and the "why."
- Manage the perception you want others to have of you.
- Be a selective perfectionist; eight out of 10 can be great.

- Be tough on issues. Be demanding. Set high standards.
- Show that you can develop and bring out the best in your people.
- Demonstrate your ability to solve problems.
- Show others that you are a team player.
- Be a positive participant at meetings.
- Be a superb communicator, oral and written.
- Be a great listener.
- Be decisive.
- Work with a sense of urgency.
- Be responsible and accountable.
- Never blame others.
- Manage by majority, not consensus.
- Leave a corporate event in the same state you walked in.
- Develop your lateral thinking abilities.
- Say and do positive things.
- Be the go-to person.
- Ensure you have strong relationships, within the company and outside it.
- Give your people credit for their accomplishments; forget "me-me."
- Celebrate success with your people.
- Give "hugs."

Those are the essential elements of real leadership. Make sure you have those skills and best practices in order to be a true leader. If you don't have and demonstrate them all, you've got work to do. Use the list above to bring out the best in your people and help them develop and mature into leaders as well.

And before you promote an individual into a leadership position, make sure they have most of the skills above. In fact, your career development plan for them should be based on their acquiring these skills and showing you that they have the ability to use them. Then go ahead and promote them, and give yourself a "hug" for that immense achievement.

Remember, leaders who lack leadership skills are usually like fish out of water; they are ill suited for the position they've had thrust upon them.

At best, they will be ineffective; at worst, they can cause a lot of damage to the organization and its people. These types of leaders, the leaders in name only, are usually fence sitters, incapable of making the decisions that are required to move the business forward.

The reality is that many people do not have the capacity, the courage, the knowledge, the confidence, or even the desire to be a leader. The truth is that every organization needs "doers" as well as leaders; the trick is learning to tell the difference between them and developing the right ones to be leaders in your business. The doers in your organization need to be told, directed, and inspired to "do"—by your leaders. And the leaders need to provide positive reinforcement to those who "do" very well. They should be commended for their efforts and their contributions. If this sounds to you like your leaders should be willing givers of recognition—of "hugs"—you are right!

True leaders, with well-developed or inherent leadership skills, exhibit the following positive qualities: courage, strength of character, persistence, determination, ability to inspire others, charisma, creativity, vision, and enthusiasm, among others. They are a positive force in the organization and can have a profound influence on the people. When considering leaders or potential leaders in your business, ask yourself the following questions:

1. Do the individuals that you're considering have a good understanding of human behavior?
2. Are they able to praise and show appreciation to people?
3. Are they able to recognize the differences in people and manage accordingly?
4. Have they demonstrated the ability and skill to properly manage people?
5. Have you seen evidence of their ability to inspire and motivate others?
6. Do they work with a sense of urgency?
7. When the proverbial fan starts turning, do they possess the courage, calm, and confidence necessary to address the situation and inspire their people to resolve it—or are they just "doers" themselves?
8. Do they have the fortitude and the brain power to make the tough decisions?

9. Do they know what needs to be done and why it needs to be done—and then are they able to effectively communicate this to their people? Remember, we called this clarity of expectations.
10. Do they know how to execute consequences when required, thus setting a standard of behavior that is clear to everyone?
11. Is their moral and ethical compass a positive one and is it in clear evidence for everyone to follow?
12. What perception have they created for themselves within the company? Is it a positive one? Do people look up to them? Are they a standard-bearer?
13. Are they emblematic of the values, the principles, and the credo of the company?
14. Are people inclined to follow them?

Here's a letter I wrote to a leader who was questioning his effectiveness in his relatively new role. It will add another dimension to what true leadership really means.

> Dear Burt,
>
> I know we talked on the phone earlier this week, but I wanted to add some thoughts for your consideration.
>
> Leadership and strength of character are best demonstrated when times are tough, when circumstances are not as we hoped they would be, when challenges hit us in the gut, when that lump in the throat just won't go away.
>
> When things are great, even the weak look strong.
>
> Having said that, there is no doubt that these are difficult times for every company and for every individual. So it's kind of normal to question yourself and wonder about your skills and talents as a leader.
>
> That humility you have is to be admired. It's good to have a mirror handy and to look into it periodically.

I'm actually glad you're doing that and I'm thrilled that you are reaching out and seeking my comments. So here goes.

I think you're a great leader with excellent leadership skills. And I say that based on the observations I've made about what you've said and what you've done since taking over the regional manager's position.

Real leaders will carefully examine their strengths, their good points, and all the good stuff they have, and then use these skills to move their business and their people forward. You've done that, and done it very well. That's leadership.

Your focus was clearly on the future and what you wanted to do to make it better for the business and better for your team. You knew it would be challenging, perhaps even daunting, but you forged ahead with a clear vision and clear expectations. That's leadership.

That has resulted in your team doing great things in the short time you've been there. People are "born again" thanks to your leadership. They have re-invented themselves in so many ways thanks to your encouragement and the real sense of caring that you have demonstrated so well. That's leadership.

Those who had thought of quitting, under the previous regime, are working harder and smarter than ever. You have given them new hope, new levels of satisfaction in their lives and a new sense of pride in who they are and what they are. That's leadership.

Thanks to you and your leadership talents, your team is generating great results. The business is in great shape. The future has never looked better. There's a sense of urgency with the team. You're seeing new initiatives and new creativity from your people. All that is a result of your leadership.

That has enabled you to virtually become a new person with a renewed level of self-confidence and a remarkable record of achievement. That's the prize of true leadership.

Indeed, the past year adds yet another building block to what is a great pattern of success for you.

Equally important, in my view, is the undeniable fact that you have discovered, created and fostered a wonderful balance between "head and heart management," which you and I have talked about.

And what makes it very special is that you've learned and applied that balance in such a short period of time. That's great leadership.

It's outstanding leadership!

I, for one, am extremely proud of you and proud of your progress and your achievements.

Kindest Regards,
George

So what exactly did Burt do to demonstrate true leadership? When he first took over the troubled region he did so with an open mind, rather than an "I know it all" approach. His notebook was clear, a blank slate; he didn't have preconceived notions about anything. He wanted to go out and discover the reality of the situation himself, because he knew that the reality would be far more powerful than gossip, hearsay, and rumors.

He wanted to hear what the members of the new team had to say. He wanted to listen to them, and listen carefully. He wanted the opportunity to ask them all kinds of questions and to hear what their answers would be. He wanted to get as close to the truth as was possible. He respected the views, the opinions, and the reality that people expressed. He didn't judge what was said. He just listened attentively.

One of the guideposts of leadership is that you can't say that you want to discover the reality of things and then judge what is being said at the same time. Listen first to what the other person is saying; think about it, digest it, analyze it; consider the other person's viewpoint and circumstances, and only then apply your own judgment on the matter.

For Burt, this process of discovery resulted in a torrent of information that no one could have predicted beforehand. Armed with these facts, he was able to create a plan of action that would rekindle team spirit, restore trust, and re-energize every member of the team. He was able to respond to the needs of his internal customers.

What's vital to note here is that his plan was created to fit the circumstances and the facts of the situation. It wasn't a technical formula that so many managers make the mistake of applying, without regard to the circumstances they face and the real needs of their people. It became very evident to Burt, once he discovered the facts, that there was a huge gap between the "head and heart" elements, so vital to any successful business. Slowly and surely, Burt demonstrated his ability to pay attention to people and what they were doing.

He looked for the positives, and then began to "hug" his people for the successful contributions they were making. He noticed their efforts, the work they did on weekends, the early arrivals and the late departures, and "hugged" his people for these things. The team developed a fresh spirit and a sense of caring they had not experienced before. They felt important, for the first time in a long time. They were acknowledged and shown a new level of respect. They began to feel a renewed sense of pride in the company and in what they were doing. The power of the "hug" is truly awesome. It's key to arriving at a balance between "head and heart."

It may sound strange at first to hear the word "hug" in business, but do not for a second let the strangeness of that word deter you from using it—metaphorically, of course—to manage your people better. And as I've written all along in this book, the "hug" principle will definitely and absolutely make you a better manager and a superb leader.

16
MANAGING THE VOICE

I believe that all of us go through life with "a voice" in our head. And the "voice" I refer to is the voice of our parents and those who were a part of our formative years. For some, it was a pleasant voice. For many others, it was not so pleasant. It was the kind that drives you crazy and just won't go away. No matter what kind of internal voice we each listen to, it still guides us; it directs our efforts, it dictates our behavior, and impacts what we do and how we do it.

In effect, we are who we are today because of "the voice" and what it tells us. That voice can turn us into killers. It can make us beautiful people. It can turn us into bullies. Or it can propel us into a life of caring and compassion. What's amazing is that the voice never leaves us. It's always there, whether we know it or not, whether we admit it or not or, in most cases, whether we realize it or not.

One of my clients heard the voice of his older brother putting him down, telling him what to do, what courses he should take, what profession he should follow, and trying to control every other aspect of his life. His mission in life was to prove his brother wrong. Instead of becoming a doctor, like his older brother wanted him to be, he went into the advertising field, set up his own company and became very successful, selling his business for millions. He proved his older brother wrong, but he stills hears his voice.

> "How do I get rid of the voice? How do I stop it from choking me up? Will I ever stop hearing it? Will I ever forget the experience? Will I ever be able to erase the hurt files that it created and that still bother me?"

NO! You can never erase the voice, and, as we discussed earlier, you can never erase the hurt files. But you can drown out the voice with one that's more positive, one that comes from within you, and one that you have the power to write the script for. Here's an example of that.

The voices I heard when I was young, and still hear, were relentlessly negative, thanks to a difficult, abusive childhood. But they motivated me to be better, to change my circumstances. Eventually, I learned to change those voices as well, to much more positive messages to myself. In fact, I now close all my motivational talks and my seminars with these words:

> "Thank you all for being here today. Throughout my childhood I was told that I was good for nothing; that I wouldn't amount to much. I hope that today I've helped some of you and proved to 'them' that I am, in fact, good for something."

I trained myself to manage the voice I heard for many years as I grew up, to turn the negative messages to positive ones—and it worked. And if I can do it, you can, too.

Throughout most of this book, we've talked about how you can be a better manager by learning and practising how to give more positive messages to your employees, how to recognize them rather than reject them—how to give them a hug. In this chapter, the focus is on you—how to give some of that love, attention, and acceptance to yourself. It's true that when others say or do something to recognize us, they can have a profound positive influence on our life. But that recognition, that hug, doesn't always have to come from an external source. If you can learn to wrap your arms around yourself sometimes, that can be a powerful source of positive energy too.

To start with, here are a few coping techniques that will help you change the negative, hurtful voice you've always heard in your head into one that's happier and more constructive.

- Keep your "mouse" away from the not-so-pleasant files. Instead, click on the positive files you'll focus on creating from this moment on. In fact, go into your mental computer right now and open a new folder called "positives."
- Starting today, create positive files. And yes, it's much easier than you think. Simply do something or say something that is positive and pleasing to others. It's that easy.
- Giving positive messages to others through your words and actions will generate positive responses directed back at you: "Thanks for doing that." "That was very kind of you." "How very thoughtful of you to consider me." "I really appreciated your card; it made my day." "You're a class act for doing that." "You really are incredible; I wish I had your tenacity." "What you did was awesome, so thanks for that," and so on.
- Every one of those responses and reactions from others indicates appreciation, acceptance, validation, and all the other good things you would have liked to hear from "the voice." Put them all in your new "positives folder."
- Say and do things that will elicit responses from others that lift you up, instead of sizing you down. For example, it's uplifting to hear a "thank you," to be acknowledged for one's kindness or act of caring.

That is completely opposite to what you've heard from "the voice," which only put you down. No matter what you did, no matter what you said, you were berated, abused, not appreciated, not accepted, intimidated, bullied, and so on and so on. The voice was one great put-down. Period.

So, since you can't eliminate the voice, you can't fix it, you can't change it, you can't get rid of it, why not come to the realization that all you can do is to replace it—replace it with the words, the actions, the kindness, the accolades, the appreciation, and the acceptance you've always wanted to hear, to feel, to experience?

You have complete control over changing the voice that plays constantly in your head. And you will eventually realize, and come to believe, that you are far better than the voice ever acknowledged you were. Is it that simple? YES, YES, YES!

Again, to repeat, since the voice cannot be erased, we have the option to replace it. Please consider and respond to the following questions.

How would you feel if you opened an envelope and read a two- or three-page letter thanking you for your help and support on something you did? What's your answer?
Feel Great ____   Terrible ____

How would you feel and how would you respond, emotionally, if a friend, or acquaintance, called you up and invited you to dinner and a hockey game, or the opera, or the ballet, or a movie, or a concert? What's your answer?
Feel Great ____   Terrible ____

How would you feel if you got a handwritten note thanking you for the ideas and suggestions you made at yesterday's meeting? What's your answer?
Feel Great ____   Terrible ____

How would you react if a colleague called you up to say that your suggestions really made a significant difference to the project being worked on? What's your answer?
Feel Great ____   Terrible ____

How would you feel if you won the "Marketing Director of the Year" award, or any other award for that matter?
Feel Great ____   Terrible ____

Any, and all, of these positive files would put a smile on your face, perhaps a lump in your throat, and would make you feel great. Any, and all, of these acknowledgments would lift you up in entirely new ways.

And here's another key point. If you as a manager do these kinds of things for the people who report to you and those who work with you, it will surely lift those people up and help them feel better, feel more accomplished and far more confident in themselves. It will also help them manage and control the voice they listen to. So much can be achieved for you and for others by this small act of recognition:

Give a Hug—Get a Hug

If you received a metaphorical hug for even the smallest action or reason, your confidence level would increase, you'd feel important, appreciated, accepted, validated, and so on. Your ego would be awakened and you'd feel terrific, certainly better than the "voice" ever made you feel.

My point is that the voice will always be with you, and one of the best ways of dealing with it, managing it, is to drown it out with a whole bunch of positive accomplishments and positive activities that put a smile on your face. Please understand: there is no technique that will ever erase the voice. *"If you can't erase, you must replace."*

17

BOOST YOUR OWN SELF-CONFIDENCE

At the core of most coaching situations is the unassailable fact that people need a major injection of confidence. In many ways, confidence, pure and simple, is the fuel that drives every human initiative. We're all trying to prove that we're good at something, that we're worthy, and that we're deserving of some accolades. Usually, that "proving" is to impress someone else—parents, family, friends, manager, community, and so on.

Since confidence is such a powerful driver, it's vital to have a method of building our own confidence. Other people won't always be around to give us confidence when we most need it and, in fact, we've seen that some people will chip away at, or completely destroy, our confidence with their negative talk and behavior. Thus, it is critical that we have a technique that enables us to build our own self-confidence.

In essence, confidence is a belief and a certainty in yourself, in what you can do, and in how you do it. I'm often asked if confidence comes with birth. My answer, without having any statistics or research to substantiate it, is that confidence is not something that people are born with. Like many other skills and talents, it is something that is nurtured and developed during the growing up years. It starts with parents, and then moves on to the teachers, school mates, friends, and the working environment that people find themselves in. Confidence is gained:

- by what people say
- by their actions
- by their efforts
- by their accomplishments
- by their contributions
- by how they are encouraged
- by how they are supported
- by how they are mentored

Confidence can be nurtured and built up to very high levels and thus can equip the individual to perform better in his or her life. However, if confidence has not been nurtured over the years, what do we do now, at this stage of our life? Let me share with you the "positives" method that has worked wonders with the people I've coached.

First, get a blank piece of paper and write down all the positive skills, talents, attributes, and traits that you have. Write down all the positive things that you are proud of, all the accomplishments you've attained and all the good things you've done.

It's a tough exercise to do. You probably have never done this before in your entire life and you may have a hard time tooting your own horn like this. No problem. Push yourself to get it started and plan to add to the list every day. Don't try to do it all at once. If you think you're stuck, seek the input of people you like and trust. Limit yourself to two weeks to get it done. You can always add to it later. Remember, only positives.

Now that you have a list of your positive qualities, skills, talents, and attributes, we need to move into what I like to call the "show me" phase of this exercise. It's similar in nature to the "Show 'em" principle we talked about earlier. I want to emphasize the importance of showing or demonstrating your skills and talents. It's just not enough to say you're good at something; it's more important that you demonstrate that skill through your actions. And you'll see why that's so vital in a few paragraphs from now.

Okay, let's move on. Beside each skill, talent and attribute on your list, I want you to outline some specific examples of how you demonstrated and applied your talent. Here's what I mean. If you have "caring" as one of your positives, write down a few examples of how you demonstrated caring. For example, "Took care of grandmother," "Helped newcomers to our church get settled in their home," whatever you did that is a clear indication of how you actually demonstrated the quality of caring. Don't just tell me you care, "show me" real, concrete examples. Actually I should say, show yourself real, concrete examples.

If you write down "resourceful," write down as many examples that you can think of that prove you are resourceful. Don't just tell me; "show me." If you say you are a whiz doing PowerPoint, "show me" examples of that skill. Don't just tell me; "show me."

Skills/Attributes	**"Show Me" Examples**
_____	_____
_____	_____
_____	_____
_____	_____

The examples you outline should prove to yourself that you have, indeed, achieved a lot; you've done a lot; you've given a lot; and so on. When they do this exercise, most people are amazed at what they've done. Most are amazed at all their positives.

That will be a tremendous boost to your own confidence. And if you're honest with yourself, you will see a well-rounded individual with much to be proud of—despite what others may think or what they have said. You've proven to yourself that you're damn good, even great, in many areas.

That's the key point of this exercise. The attributes and the examples of actually demonstrating them are proof positive of your own character, of your own accomplishments, of your own personal growth and development over the years. That's what I call real self-confidence. It doesn't rely on what others say but rather on your own actions, your own words, your own deeds—in other words, your own "stuff."

I understand that it's very important to hear praise and appreciation from others, which is a major component of this book. But at the same time, I also need to stress the importance of self-confidence, the kind of confidence that comes from within, that comes from *self*. When you look in the mirror, I want you to see a huge dose of confidence that you have developed and nurtured throughout your life, and that you are very proud of.

The reason I'm stressing this point of self is that too many people, if not most, tend to rely on others to tell them they are good, that they are smart, that they are competent, and so on. It's nice acknowledgment, no doubt, but self means self—you, and no one else. Self is foundational. It's genuine. It's real—and that's what I want for you.

When confidence increases, the tasks of life are that much easier, be they in the sports field, in investing, in golf, in acting, in just about everything. That's why we have the expression "they make it look so easy." When you've gained confidence in yourself, when you are accomplished and confident in doing something, it will most definitely be easy to do. So get busy doing the exercise:

Skills/Attributes	*"Show Me" Examples*

18

MAKE "WHY NOT?" YOUR STRATEGIC FOCUS

I was asked by a client, now my dear friend Michel, if he might review parts of my manuscript. He was surprised to learn about my past, inspired by what he read, and then he asked, "How is it possible that a person who was so abused and mistreated could make it in this crazy world? How did you become so successful? You need to answer that question in your book." So here's the answer: *"Why not?"*

I've always had what I call a strategic focus in my life or, if you prefer, a roadmap, a plan, a goal, that would help me focus on what I wanted in my life and why. I firmly believe and coach people on that principle.

You can only succeed if you really want to succeed.

You can only achieve if you really want to achieve.

You can only be happy if you really want to be happy.

You can only be better if you really want to be better.

Let me explain how that worked for me and by that example, indicate how having a strategic focus will help you immensely. As an abused child in the ghetto, my only thought was, "I have to get out of this place." That was my first-ever strategy, even though I didn't even know how to spell that word at the time. I just know that I'd get up every morning and that phrase would ring in my head. The ringing got louder and louder as I grew up fighting my way out of the place I was in.

The next strategy I created for myself, again without really knowing what a strategy meant, was how I went about getting my first job right after graduating from McGill University. It was as a sales representative with Johnson & Johnson. After a relentless number of phone calls, the National Sales Director finally agreed to see me. I had to go for an interview and was shaking for days before. It was to be my first-ever interview. I had no one to talk to about the interview, no one to seek advice from. I was alone, as I was throughout my childhood.

So as I walked through the streets of the ghetto, I kept thinking, "I just have to get this job. I don't know a thing about selling but I have to sell myself. There must be dozens of people applying for this job; forget 'em, the job is mine. I just have to distinguish myself from all the others. I'll show 'em; I'm gonna be different. I'm gonna be special. I'm gonna make this person hire me on the spot; I'm not going to take no for an answer. I'm gonna dazzle him."

That was my focus. And I decided that my point of differentiation was that I would offer to work for three months without pay, in order to prove to him that I was a good worker, that I was prepared to do anything he wanted—and that I could learn how to sell. As crazy as that sounded, as unconventional an approach as it was, I just kept thinking—*Why not?*

The day of the interview arrived. I walked into his office, shaking, nervous, and very unsure of what would happen. All I was confident about was what I would say at the opening of the interview:

> *"Good Morning. Thank you very much, sir, for seeing me. I just graduated from McGill University with a Bachelor's degree in business and psychology. It took me six years to graduate because I didn't have enough money and I had to leave to get a job to put myself through university.*
>
> *"I want this job as a sales representative but I must be honest with you—I don't know a thing about selling. What I do know is that I'm willing to learn and be the best sales person you've ever hired.*

And in order to get there, sir, I'm willing to work for you for three months without pay. I'll do anything and everything you ask of me, and you'll see how hard I work and how quickly I can learn things. Three months without paying me a single cent and I'll prove to you that you made a great decision to hire me."

He looked at me puzzled, even startled at my offer, "Are you serious?"

"Yes sir, I'm very serious. I have no experience. All I have right now is a piece of paper from McGill, which only proves that I passed a bunch of exams. I want this job and the only way I can prove to you that I deserve it is to work for you and show you how good I am, and it's not fair that you pay me for that. If after the three months you think I've earned the job, then I'll be the happiest person in the world when you make it official. If I haven't earned the right to have this job, we'll shake hands and I'll be on my way, no hard feelings."

"Okay, young man, give me a day or so to think about this and I'll get back to you."

"Thank you, sir. I look forward to your call and pray that it will be a positive one for me."

Now I was really shaking. I could hardly walk out of the Johnson & Johnson head office, but I did, wondering how crazy I was. Or maybe, just maybe, I had just learned what it was to be focused on a strategy, on an approach, on a decision that you make and stick to. That's not so crazy. After all, who has the perfect answer, the right answer? And I was alone with no one to ask and no one to give me that perfect answer.

I walked for miles north on Pie IX Street, wondering and wondering, reliving the interview in my head a thousand times. Sleep that night? Not a wink. The phone rang at 9:30 the next morning. I picked it up and listened.

"Thank you so much, sir. I'll be at your office at eight o'clock tomorrow." Wow.

The point of the story is that the power of "Why Not?" thinking is truly immense. While many will ask "why," the greatest achievers always ask—"why not?" So if you want to be a great leader, a great person, a great whatever, make "why not" thinking your guidepost, your strategic focus.

- Distinguish yourself from the others in the waiting room of life.
- Don't just talk about being different, make a difference.
- Don't just talk about being better, do better.
- Don't just think outside the box, do outside the box.
- Don't accept the status quo. Your responsibility as a human being is to make things better.
- Constantly ask yourself, Why not?

That why-not thinking, that strategy, that focus, led to the following list of first-ever achievements that I'm very proud to say I created and initiated in my corporate career. With your indulgence, please allow me to highlight these to prove the point that you really can do anything if you put your mind to it and invest the effort to make success happen.

"Why not" have the first-ever window displays containing only Johnson's Baby Powder all over the city of Montreal? "Why not" run the first-ever Johnson's Baby Pack promotion on radio every morning, without paying the station a cent, by giving a Baby Pack to a caller? And "why not" create a Baby Pack in the first place, containing all of the Johnson's baby products in it?

I won the Sales Representative of the Year Award, even though I had the smallest territory in the Montreal area. I beat out the other representatives who had much larger accounts, like Steinberg's and IGA and Provigo. They couldn't believe it. I just said to myself at the start of the year, "Why not?"

The typical approach may well have been, how can I possibly go up against Steinberg's, which, at the time in 1968, was Quebec's largest food retailer. My account was Leduc & Leduc, a small 10-store drug chain. The odds were against me. At least that's what everybody else thought. I knew how to deal with odds. The odds were really against me in the ghetto but I did get out. Same principle. Have a strategy. Focus on it. Think, why not? And do it. Period.

When I was promoted to the position of assistant to the product group director, basically a "Boy Friday," run-here-run-there type of job, I had the same why-not thinking in my head: I knew I could make a difference; I knew that I could make things better; I knew I could distinguish myself in a real, tangible manner. "Why not?"

A few weeks after I got the new job, my boss approached me and asked if I would be able to make a presentation on J-Cloth Towels at the upcoming national sales meeting, just three weeks away. Three weeks? "Why not?" was my immediate answer.

- "Why not" have four colors of J-Cloth Towels, instead of just two?
- "Why not" have an assorted pack of J-Cloth Towels instead of just one color?
- "Why not" have wedding gowns made in each of the four new J-Cloth colors?
- "Why not" have bikinis made out of J-Cloth Towels?
- "Why not" have boutonnieres made out of J-Cloth Towels?
- "Why not" have a Mariachi band launch the new products?
- "Why not" have fireworks going off as people walked into the room?
- "Why not" take condoms out from behind the pharmacy counter and put them on display in the front of the store—huge end-aisle displays, in fact?
- "Why not" have a "Get 3 Free" condom promotional package?
- "Why not" create a no-belts, no-pins, no-strings-attached feminine napkin, that would simply stick to a woman's panty, instead of all those other things they had to use—and "why not" call it Stayfree?
- "Why not" be the first on TV with feminine hygiene advertising?
- "Why not" have 67 speeches in the same day, from 8:00 a.m. to 4:00 p.m.?

I am very proud that I did all of the above. And I accomplished all these things, and so much more, simply because I asked myself over and over again, "Why not?"

Why-not thinking and personal focus are very powerful motivators that will drive you to achieve great things. Try it. Why not?

19

WHAT WOULD YOUR LICENSE PLATE SAY?

Let me ask you a seemingly strange question. What does your personal license plate have written on it? Please note that I said "personal," not your actual car license plate.

I know what you're thinking: what the heck does a license plate have to do with anything in my life, in my work, and in the relationships I have? Don't panic. I have a good reason for asking the question.

Think about this for a minute: every state, every province, issues motor vehicle license plates. Each license plate has a saying on it: "Yours to Discover" (Ontario), "The Sunshine State" (Florida), "Show-Me State" (Missouri), "Wild and Wonderful" (West Virginia), and so on. Presumably, these sayings are designed to describe a significant characteristic of the province or state.

I like the fact that license plates have sayings on them. And I like the idea even more if we could apply it to individuals. It can be a guidepost for what you do in your life, a personal slogan, a clear statement of your own objective, your purpose, your driving force. It allows people to see what you stand for.

I know, it's not something most people think of. In fact, you should see the strange looks I get when I first mention the idea. But it's an interesting notion, isn't it?

What would you want people to remember about you? What would you like them to say about you?

What would you like your license plate to read? Write it down.

_____

The saying on your license plate provides you with a definitive way to manage your life, manage your work, and manage your relationships. Your personal "license plate" gives you a clear and succinct vision for your life. It describes guidelines for future actions and activities, and how you want to conduct them from here on in.

Isn't that amazing—a vision, a future roadmap, a clear strategy to help you conduct your personal and professional affairs? It's kind of a crazy notion isn't it? It's off-the-wall isn't it? Maybe it is; but then again, why not?

In case you're interested, my personal license plate reads, "He Helped Me." Helping people is the single biggest mission in my life. It's my raison d'être. Whatever I do, it has to have a "help" component in it. Writing this book is all about helping, for example. My business cards read, "35 Years of Helping People;" my tombstone will read, "He Helped Me."

Over the years I've learned that if I help others first, they will shower me with the attention, the appreciation, and all those other good things I craved as a child. In fact it's helped minimize the pain and frustration of all the "hurt files" I've had to endure.

Your personal license plate should sum up your vision, your key goal—the one quintessential thing that guides you, motivates you, and fulfills you in just about everything you do. Distilling your life's strategy into such a concise expression can help you clarify your life's objective, your life's purpose. And if it guides you to do more of what you love the most and is most important to you, then you can be happier and more fulfilled than you ever thought possible.

20

MY BEST FRIEND, GEORGE

I studied Shakespeare at McGill University, but along the way I discovered and fell in love with George Bernard Shaw. He became "My Best Friend, George."

As I said earlier, all I ever wanted in my life was a "hug." That's all any child really wants. But I just didn't get one, for the many reasons I've already mentioned. Battered and abused, I made it my ambition to get out of the ghetto—somehow, some way, some day. Nothing was going to stop me from attaining the objective of turning that dream into reality.

There was only one problem: I didn't know *how* I was going to do it. After all, for six days a week I had the challenge of trying to avoid being beaten up by my grandmother. On the seventh day, I found peace and tranquility and appreciation at the St. Nicholas Church. But I was still in the ghetto.

My dream of getting out was intact. My resolve to get out was like hardened steel. My focus was singular. I just didn't know how to do it. And then like a bolt of lightning it hit me, a passage in one of George Bernard Shaw's plays, *Mrs. Warren's Profession* (1893):

People are always blaming their circumstances for who they are.
I don't believe in circumstances.

The people who get on in this world are the people who get up and look for the circumstances they need to be successful.

And if they can't find them, they create them.

Wow! That resonated with me. That put everything about my life into perspective; it captured the essence of how I was feeling, what I was thinking. In a few short lines it gave me the direction I so desperately needed. And it prevented me from doing damage to myself, which I must admit had crossed my mind several times in that damn ghetto.

In just a few short lines, Mr. Shaw understood me and gave me the major how-to for my future—and my life. I suddenly realized that I had to create the circumstances I needed to get out of the ghetto. It was up to me, no one else was going to help me—no one. And no one did. I had to do everything for myself, and it's been that way all my life. I learned to be self-reliant, to be resourceful, to take risks, to drive myself to be better each day, to take initiatives, to be decisive, not to wait for others, to be different, to distinguish myself through positive words and actions, and to say and do things that would make me successful and happy and all those good things.

It's amazing what happens when you have a direction—when you operate with a strategy in mind, rather than running around aimlessly, just fooling yourself and pretending to know what you're doing. George Bernard Shaw was the only person to provide me with that direction. I became acutely aware of what I had to do, why I had to do it, and how I was going to do it. Equally important, I had a roadmap that would guide my every effort and every action.

All that and more, thanks to Mr. Shaw. That's how powerful his words were to me. They really saved my life and pointed me in a positive direction. That's how he became—and still is today—"My Best Friend, George."

It's worth repeating his inspiring words:

People are always blaming their circumstances for who they are.
I don't believe in circumstances.

The people who get on in this world are the people who get up and look for the circumstances they need to be successful.

And if they can't find them, they create them.

Please, go create the circumstances you need!

Create circumstances that ensure you keep people on your agenda; that give you the opportunity to lift others up and add value to their lives; that enable you to give them a hug, so that, in turn, you are given the hug that will sustain you and make you feel great. That will reward you with the inspiration to make things around you much better and much more satisfying. Remember the power you have to give others a hug, in every sense of that word. I promise that you will enjoy life a lot more and you'll bring out the full potential you have to do more and to derive more from your work and from your personal and family life.

"GIMME A HUG"

No doubt a rather strange title for a book that focuses on people management in both the workplace and in our daily interactions. Several friends and colleagues suggested I use a different title but I held firm because "All I ever wanted in my life was a hug," was the refrain I heard from all the people I've had the honor to help over the past 35 years.

So I started the book with the question, What's This "Hug" Stuff All About? I trust that by now that question has been clearly explained and will help you incorporate "hugs" into the manner and style of how you manage and interact with people, be they at work, at home, wherever. I also hope that I've demonstrated how this thing called "a hug" is at the essence of human behavior and the central role it plays in people's lives.

The "hug" is the ultimate recognition.

It is the opposite of rejection.

It explains why bullies are what and who they are.

It helps to understand why perfectionists put themselves through so much anguish.

It is a chief catalyst for improving the bottom line of any business.

It's the key to creating a positive working environment.

It's the root cause of fostering a culture of success.

And it is certainly one of the prime ways for you to maximize your potential as a leader and as a human being, and derive the full satisfaction you deserve from life.

"Gimme a Hug" is the prime need I've listened to. Of course, it wasn't a physical hug the people I worked with and coached craved, but rather a metaphorical one. That was the starting point of this book. The end of this book implores you to create opportunities to "hug" everyone you interact with from this moment forward, and in doing so, to derive and enjoy a new level of satisfaction.

ACKNOWLEDGMENTS

With Much Love and Appreciation To:

Anthony, Andrea, Andy, Alex, Ash, Ainsley, Anna, Audin, Barbara, Barry, Brian, Bryan, Brad, Beverly, Bill, Bob, Burt, Candace, Chanel, Chad, Cathy, Christian, Christine, Chris, Claudio, Craig, Carina, Chuck, Carmen, Doreen, David, Darlene, Deborah, Debbie, Don, Diana, Denise, Dawn, Dennis, Dan, Elizabeth, Ernest, Edward, Eddie, Feroz, Glenn, Gilda, Greg, Gerry, Hannah, Henry, Hank, Iram, Jeffrey, Jason, Joe, Judith, Judy, Jerry, John, Joel, Joan, Janet, Jean-Marc, Jean-Daniel, Jenn, Jonathon, Jennifer, Jeremy, Kelly, Kathryn, Kate, Karen, Kevin, Koray, Laila, Lynn, Laurens, Laina, Luigi, Lisa, Lou, Maurice, Malcolm, Marianne, Mary, Michelle, Maureen, Michel, Mark, Marc, May, Matt, Michael, Mike, Margie, Mathieu, Mario, Neville, Nadine, Nicole, Nick, Nicolas, Naseem, Peter, Percy, Pierre, Perry, Peg, Paul, Philippe, Phil, Rob, Robert, Ronald, Ronnie, Richard, Stan, Stacey, Stephane, Sandro, Sandy, Sonia, Serge, Sophia, Susan, Scott, Steven, Stephanie, Sylvain, Stephen, Sharon, Tanya, Tony, Tyler, Terry, Tom, Victor, Vivian, Vince, Vincent, Walter, Wilma, and many more that I've coached in my 35 years.

Thank you for sharing your stories with me. To all of you, I want you to know that it has been a true honor and a privilege to have been given the opportunity to help you in the ways that only you know about. I am so proud of you and the incredible progress all of you have made in your careers and in your personal lives.

I truly love every one of you. What we shared together was an incredible journey, a truly remarkable one that was genuine, sincere and honest in every way. We cried a lot together, but we also laughed a lot together. I dedicate this book to you. I want you to know how much you helped to enrich my life. I thank you so deeply for that and for the privilege of working with you.

And to my departed friends, Don, Fred, and Peter N, I miss you so much and I hope that you can hear me say "thanks" from that peaceful place I know you're in.

And at the end of the day, we can all look back and say that we made great discoveries about ourselves. We learned so much. We are certainly better today than we were yesterday—and, yes, we gave each other a great big hug! Because all we ever asked for in our life was, "Gimme a hug."

I also want to express my appreciation and gratitude to Andrea and Karen, for their wisdom, expertise, guidance, the odd kick in the butt, their additions and deletions and all the "good stuff" they gave me.

A very special thanks to Karen for "being with me." You were the support, the inspiration, and the "hugger" I desperately needed to complete this decades-long project. Your "hug" motivated me to take it to the finish line, and for that, I thank you. Oh and one more note please, Karen, just to rub it in, you truly helped make this book "More Better" than it was. (She doesn't like the phrase, More Better.)

I also want to recognize and express much appreciation to my sisters, May and Diana, and to my wonderful niece, Tanya, who all helped me with this book in so many ways they know about.

And of course, the biggest "hug" I've ever received has been from my wife, Marlene. We've been together for more than 50 years, a true testimony to the loving and wonderful relationship we've had.

Marlene has stood by me every step of my crazy ways. Always there during that period of my working incessantly to achieve the strategic goals I set for myself and set for us as a couple. Marlene demonstrated incredible patience as I re-invented myself to pursue dreams and make them reality.

She sacrificed a lot for our relationship and for that, I am eternally grateful. She's been by my side throughout the many challenges and joys of life. And she's done that while struggling with and managing the health challenges of MS. Marlene is a truly remarkable human being, in every respect. I love her dearly.

Thanks Sanadee, for all the "hugs" you've given me, and all the hugs we've shared.

Photo credit: Diana Kouri and May Kouri

ABOUT THE AUTHOR

George Kouri graduated from McGill University in Business and Psychology and spent the next twelve years developing a successful business career, eventually becoming a Senior Executive within the Johnson & Johnson family of companies. After leaving corporate life, George then used his management and business development experience to create a unique and dynamic Executive Coaching business.

Since 1979, George's purpose has been focused on a singular objective: to bring out the best in people and, in so doing, to generate outstanding business results and allow people to reach new heights of personal and professional satisfaction. This powerful combination has enabled George to create an unrivaled reputation for "helping people." He has assisted individuals across various industries in developing effective leadership and people management techniques. His unique style and coaching method brings out the full potential of people and builds their confidence.

George has an amazing ability to endear himself to others and to motivate and inspire them to "be better than they think they are." His passion, indeed his life, is all about people and the tremendous potential they have. He has a solid, practical, and professional grasp of what it takes to bring out the best in people.

His style is open and direct; he respects the differences in individuals; he facilitates the dynamics of team effort; and he coaches people to be wildly successful. This book encapsulates exactly how "wildly successful" can be achieved.

Of the many accomplishments he is proud of, George cites . . .

"The hundreds of letters of thanks I've received over the years."

www.ingramcontent.com/pod-product-compliance
Lightning Source LLC
Chambersburg PA
CBHW051640170526
45167CB00001B/272